A CUP OF COMFORT®
Book of
BIBLE PROMISES

Stories That Celebrate
God's Encouraging Words

Edited by
James Stuart Bell
and Susan B. Townsend

Avon, Massachusetts

Published by
Adams Media, a division of F+W Media, Inc.
57 Littlefield Street, Avon, MA 02322 U.S.A.

ISBN 13: 978-1-59869-855-8

Printed in the United States of America.

Library of Congress Cataloging-in-Publication Data
is available from the publisher.

Contents

Acknowledgments

To Gabriel, Emily, Dylan, Connor, and Owen. SBT

To Brian Masserelli. JSB

As always, our heartfelt thanks go to Paula Munier, Sara Stock, Brendan O'Neill, and Matthew Glazer, whose wisdom, guidance, and encouragement made this book possible.

Introduction

When my friends and I were very young, promises were made swiftly and passionately, and we usually demonstrated our sincerity with the symbolic gesture of crossing our hearts and hoping to die. Often, these solemn vows were just as quickly forgotten in the heat of petty disagreements or amended loyalties. However, I grew up in a home where the truth was held in the highest regard, and it wasn't long before I was determined to follow the example set by my parents. They kept their promises, not only to each other and their children, but also to the rest of the people in their lives.

My parents also introduced me to the promises of God. As a child, I found them comforting and encouraging, but when I left home I fell under the delusion that I was the mistress of my destiny, and those promises lost their power to inspire and console. Eventually, they became only words in a book I used to read.

In the years that followed, I failed miserably at managing life on my own. People I trusted betrayed me, and I began to doubt that anyone was capable of keeping a promise. Worse yet, I lost sight of my childhood determination to follow through on the promises I made which resulted in a suffocating accumulation of guilt. It never occurred to me that I was asking myself—and others—to perform the impossible.

It took a tragic accident to breathe life back into the Biblical promises I had learned as a child. At the time, all I could think about was the possible loss of my beloved husband. Suddenly, I began to pray with a faith-filled trust I didn't think I possessed any longer. I recited the twenty-third Psalm over and over, and as the hours passed, I became filled with the conviction that God was listening. It was then I realized that He had always been listening, even during the many years when I had been silent. He had never forsaken me, even when I pushed Him away. He had kept His promises.

That was the beginning of my voyage of discovery, and the end of my futile journey on the dead-end road of self-reliance. Now, my Bible has become far more than mere words. It is an inspired, inerrant, and infallible book of God's instructions to me on how to live my life, a message of love from the Lord filled with countless promises to see me through every situation from tragedy to triumph.

We hope you will be encouraged, entertained, and blessed by this collection of stories from people sharing their experiences with God's promises. From the grieving daughter God led to forgive her estranged sister after their father died to the harried mother who found proof of God's love at a local garage sale, each contributor has demonstrated how we can all trust in God's promises. People from all walks of life, in every possible circumstance, have discovered that these promises are as relevant today as they were thousands of years ago. If you're new to God's word, or unfamiliar with His promises, we pray you'll be moved to discover what He has in store for your life, too.

—*Susan B. Townsend*

Amazing Grace
in Glasgow

*But even greater is God's wonderful grace
and his gift of righteousness, for all who
receive it will live in triumph over sin and
death through this one man Jesus Christ.*

Romans 5:17

I stepped away from the dusty surface of the chalk-board and took a deep breath. Was I really in Glasgow, Scotland, thousands of miles from home? And did these seventh-graders still have as much trouble understanding me as I did understanding them? A dark-haired girl in the front row raised her hand, "'Scuze me, Miss, but I can't find me jotter."

Her what? My mind catapulted through the possibilities. *Jotter? Like to jot down something. Oh, I know—her journal. She can't find her journal. Aha!* With a sigh of relief, I squatted down next to the worn desk and picked up a bound book with a colorful cover lounging on the floor near the aisle.

She smiled at me as I handed it to her. From his perch at the back of the room, my supervising teacher gave me a slight nod. Wow, I needed that. After weeks of trying to adjust to a new culture, language, and environment, relief washed over me.

Three months earlier, when my plane touched down in Glasgow, my only instructions were to look for a man holding a sign with my name. After awkward introductions, we searched for my suitcase, but it was nowhere to be found. The perky customer service employee said it was probably on a plane headed back to the states. I couldn't help but think maybe that's where I should have been, too.

With only the clothes on my back, I set off for St. Andrew's College, where I would be staying during my overseas student teaching adventure. My first glimpse revealed a brown stucco building built into the side of a hill. The dormitories looked like giant cardboard boxes, some hugging the rise, some jutting out. Rain spattered the windshield, and the driver from the college told me I should get used to cloudy, windy, and damp weather. At least his forecast matched my mental outlook.

Alone in my dorm room, I decided to talk to God about all of the things I thought were wrong with my situation. I listed my grievances and gripes, all the time wondering if He was near, even though I was so far from all that was familiar.

I did get my suitcase, but whatever I had decided to pack back in Pennsylvania didn't seem to offer much help at St. Augustine's Secondary School. There was so much to learn, starting with a multitude of words I had never heard before—and all spoken so rapidly, I just stood there with my mouth hanging open. The first time I heard a teacher call a student a "cheeky monkey," I almost burst out laughing. I regained my composure quickly when I realized the instructor was genuinely angry about the child's behavior.

When a student was threatened with a "punishment exercise" because he was disrupting the class, I thought the teacher wanted him to do jumping jacks in the aisle. Imagine my surprise when the teacher handed the offender a packet of papers on which he had to write "I will not disrupt the class" 500 times.

Every day brought new adjustments. Some were small, such as when I tried to buy a bag of plain potato chips, and I was faced with choices like pickled onion, prawn cocktail, and roast beef—none of which sounded even remotely appealing.

There were major changes, too. I soon learned that God was pushing me way out of my comfort zone. Back in the states, I attended college in a tiny town nestled in the Allegheny Mountains. Now, I had to find my way around a crowded, bustling city. Social interaction revolved around drinking, smoking, and hanging out in pubs, but with a family history of alcoholism, I stayed on the fringes and made few friends.

At times, homesickness overwhelmed me. I just wanted something familiar, and I craved my old routine, friends, and family. God made it clear that I needed to stop clinging to what I had left behind and embrace the new opportunities I had been given. I started traveling on the weekends, determined to enjoy the countryside and learn more about the history of Scotland. After renting a car and learning to drive on the other side of the road, I headed out to the Highlands.

Shy, black-faced sheep with newborn lambs dotted the countryside. I drove through low, rugged, thorny moors, only to enter endless green fields dappled with brilliant, golden-yellow blossoms. Mountain waterfalls gushed by the side of the road, and I laughed at cows with long, shaggy hair hanging in their eyes. I saw my first real castle, and when I touched the cool stone walls, I daydreamed about the knights and ladies who had lived there long ago.

On one adventure, not long after leaving the bustling city, I drove through a hard curve on a lonely country road. I glanced over to my left and standing in the middle of a field was a bagpipe player, dressed in the tartan of his clan. As I walked across the meadow, I recognized that he was playing "Amazing Grace." His passion and intensity showed on his face, and as the last notes of the song faded away, I felt as though a blessing had been said over me. I was desperately in need of God's presence and His peace, and at that moment, I felt certain He was with me—even in Scotland, thousands of miles from home.

My last few days at St. Augustine's Secondary School linger like photographs in my mind. The faculty threw a party for me, gave me gifts, and teased me about my awkward attempts to think and act like a Scot. The students created a book of poetry and made me promise to carry it back to the states and share it with other kids. I did bring their project back with me, but I also carried much more in my heart.

God's rewards came in unexpected forms while I struggled in Scotland: the giggles of students who loved my "accent," although I grew to love theirs even more; the beauty of a land that God's hands sculpted with careful precision and craftsmanship; and the endless kindness of strangers turned friends.

—*Laurie Modrzejewski*

Those Who Can't Build Towers

Each time he said, "My grace is all you need. My power works best in weakness." So now I am glad to boast about my weaknesses, so that the power of Christ can work through me. That's why I take pleasure in my weaknesses, and in the insults, hardships, persecutions, and troubles that I suffer for Christ. For when I am weak, then I am strong.

2 Corinthians 12:9–10

His pudgy baby hand, unusually large for a two-year-old, struggled to comply with the request of the smiling woman in front of him. But the smooth wooden blocks would not remain stacked. As soon as he placed more than one on top of the other, they tilted and tumbled. A frown creased his forehead, and he gave a whisper of a sigh. The examiner recognized the obvious signs of frustration, and she scooped the blocks into a bag. "We'll put these away for now," she said in a cheerful voice. Her smile faded as she jotted down some notes on her clipboard.

I knew what the notes would say. A degree and seven years of teaching had filled my brain with the psychobabble used by psychologists in the field of education—phrases such as "developmentally delayed," "cognitive impairment," and "special needs." Those were the terms they tossed about like so many multicolored balls. The words may have suited their clipboards, but they did not fit my son, even if he could not build towers.

David entered this world a month early. As he slid into the doctor's waiting hands, I caught a glimpse of a tiny, almost purple baby, and I heard the doctor pleading softly. "Come on, little fella, breathe, breathe." At last we heard the welcome wail, but instead of being laid in my waiting arms, he was whisked away to be tested, monitored, and placed in a special incubator.

Tears filled my eyes as I succumbed to the exhaustion of giving birth and concern for my newborn son. My husband and I knew children were, indeed, a gift from God. We had waited eight years for our oldest son, Ben. Now, as the medical personnel poked, prodded, and examined my baby, I gulped back the tears and clutched my husband's strong hand. We prayed together, thanking God for David and asking for His grace over our new baby's health.

Thankfully, tests revealed that David's heart and lungs were fully developed. After a few days in the hospital, he came home to our little white farmhouse. During his first weeks at home, he ate well, slept well, and grew like a weed. We knew he was growing from our frequent visits to the doctor's office. David seemed plagued with so many minor medical conditions that we jokingly called him "Murphy's child"—if anything could go wrong, it would. He had frequent ear infections, various skin conditions, and chronic congestion.

As the months went by, we became anxious about his development. At one year of age, he still could not walk or talk. We were told, "Stop comparing him to Ben. David has his own developmental schedule." I wanted to believe that. I knew David was bright. He loved books and stories, responded well to simple directions, and had a sunny, loving personality that made him a favorite with friends and family. But at age two, he had just learned to walk and his vocabulary was limited to a few one-syllable words. I contacted the local area education agency that provides services for children through the local school districts, and they agreed to test David.

Subsequent testing qualified him for an in-home instructor once a week, and I intensified my own work with him. I studied our language: how words can be broken into parts and how we use our tongues, lips, and mouths to form sounds. Then I taught David how to form the words he needed to communicate. Swimming lessons and outdoor play were provided to strengthen his muscles. We also enrolled him in a preschool two days a week.

David did grow and develop, just not at the rate of his peers. Although he was tall for his age, he was awkward, uncoordinated, and sometimes found simple tasks impossible. There was no doubt he was delayed, but inwardly, David had a spirit that wasn't restricted by weak muscles. When he was four years old, he told me he had asked Jesus into his heart, and he never wavered from that decision. He possessed a love for God's word and always hurried to hear our nightly Bible story. He had the gift of compassion and was unusually kind to others. This constantly amazed me because David was often teased and taunted for what he could not do. In spite of being on the receiving end of childhood cruelty, David reacted with a love that could only be the grace of God.

His first two years of school were spent at a small, private school. It was a wonderful, sheltered environment, and he thrived. He learned to read and was finally able to read his own beloved stories. Math was more difficult, but we worked at home drilling facts and finding ways to work with numbers so they had meaning.

When David was seven, he was given a diagnosis that made all the medical puzzle pieces fit together. He had been complaining of his foot "going to sleep," and we found ourselves visiting the office of a pediatric neurologist. He told us that David had very mild cerebral palsy—brain damage that occurs before birth. In David's case, the muscles of his right leg had tightened, pulling his foot into an unnatural position. He would eventually need surgery to correct the deformity, but they would wait until his feet had finished growing. The brain damage had also caused his learning difficulties and motor problems. Although the diagnosis was difficult to hear, we finally knew what we needed to do. We would put a support system in place so David could reach the potential we knew he had.

When my husband Gary's job required us to move, I enrolled our three children in the local public school. It was much larger than their previous private school, and I braced myself for the academic challenges David would face. At our first parent teacher conference, I heard the remarks that would be repeated over and over again throughout his schooling. "He's not a top student but he tries so hard. He always asks if he doesn't understand something. Math is difficult but he never gives up. He is so friendly and gets along with everyone." What more could any parent want?

As children increase in size and age, competition increases and winning the game rises in importance. David's hero, his brother Ben, excelled both academically and athletically. I couldn't help but worry how Ben's performance would affect David, especially since he wanted to try everything Ben did. So we let him, and David excelled in his own quiet way. He was picked for teams, even an all-star team, because he never complained about what position he played, or how often he got up to bat. He just loved to play. In high school, when football became too competitive, he was the team's manager. He was on the high school wrestling team for almost two years before he had his first winning match, but he never gave up.

David's "give it all I've got" and servant attitude did not go unnoticed in his high school. At the graduation awards ceremony, when students received honors for outstanding scholarship and leadership skills, he was presented with the award for school spirit.

David is now a young man living on his own. He is a responsible worker, both at his job and his church. He never managed to build great towers of wooden cubes, but if God has a clipboard for David, it surely lists words like integrity, love, and character. With the strength of God's grace given to him, David has built a man.

—Susan Lawrence

Who's in Charge Here?

The faithful love of the Lord never ends!
His mercies never cease. Great is his faithfulness;
his mercies begin afresh each morning.

Lamentations 3:22–23

I stood in the middle of my office, staring at mountains of cardboard boxes and dozens of file folders strewn about the room. I grabbed photos, mugs, a vase, and a mouse pad and jammed them into the boxes as I fought back my tears and tried to remain focused—one drawer at a time. I was cleaning out my office because I had just been laid off after twenty-two years.

A large part of my identity was tied to this company. Almost half of my life had been spent here. Where else would I go, what else would I do? As I faced the grim reality of unemployment, I tried to think positively. After all, I had several months of severance, including benefits. I had gone back to school as an adult learner only a few years before and completed my bachelor's degree. I was intelligent, hard working, and possessed a diverse range of skills and experience. Surely, I could find a new job.

After the initial shock wore off, I began to enjoy my unexpected "vacation." I could keep up with the laundry. I was able to have dinner on the table every night when my husband got home and fix his lunch for him to take to work each day. "When you go back to work," he said, "I'm going to miss all this."

I tried to make light of the situation. "Well, if I don't find a job, then you may have all this every day—while we're living in a tent!"

Despite my worries, I knew I should count my blessings. My husband had two minor surgeries during my lay off, which meant I could take care of him without missing any work. I had time to host a Christmas open house for our neighbors. During the gathering, a woman named Chris told me she worked at the local community college. She recommended that I come into human resources sometime to see if there were any openings. I filed this in the back of my mind, planning to follow up on her suggestion.

For the first few months, I had a part-time job and hoarded my salary like precious nuts for the winter. I figured I had plenty of time to find a job, but I thought it might be wise to put away some extra money, just in case. As the months dragged on, I realized job hunting had changed dramatically from the days when I was in my twenties. There was a new set of rules, and I didn't know what they were anymore.

I felt as if my job applications were vanishing into a black abyss. I might submit twelve online applications a week and never hear back from anyone. Or, I would receive an automated e-mail in my mailbox that read, "Thanks for applying. We've received your application and will review it. If you meet our needs at this time, we will contact you." But they never did.

A spirit of fear and doubt started to shadow me from the moment I woke up, and my self-esteem began to suffer. Every time I looked at the calendar, I panicked. I was stricken with the "what if" disease and frantically made contingency plans. What would we do if I didn't find a job? What if I found one, but it paid significantly less than what I had been earning? Well-meaning friends quoted statistics on how hard it was for older workers to find jobs in today's market. When had I become an "older" worker? I finally understood the need for age discrimination laws.

I reminded God of my predicament daily. Obviously, he had forgotten about me—and my family's needs. Couldn't he see I was responsible for helping to support my family? I had to find a job, and soon. I widened my search to include menial entry-level jobs. I sat by the phone like a lovesick teenager. I did everything possible, but God wasn't cooperating with my plan at all. What was going on?

I recognized the toll my predicament was taking on my family. "If you don't find a job, am I still going to be able to go to college?" my daughter asked. I promised her we would find a way although, secretly, I doubted our ability to do it. I knew my husband prayed, but he made little effort to discuss the problem. We had been married for just a year, and my lack of a job was proving to be a major stressor for our young marriage.

One day, I realized I had been trusting in my own ability to fix the situation, and my eyes were opened to my prideful foolishness. I thought of the Israelites on the banks of the Red Sea with the Egyptians approaching rapidly. If I had been there, I would have been feverishly building a raft instead of trusting in God for deliverance. Now, my quest for self-sufficiency had allowed everything to spiral out of control. I prayed earnestly. "God, forgive me for not trusting in You. Let Your will be done and let Your glory be revealed. You know my needs, and You have promised to meet them. Help me to trust You. Help me to find the job You want for me." I felt a sense of peace immediately. I had no idea what the future held, but I knew I was no longer in charge.

I continued my search: making contacts, filling out applications, and following up on potential leads. However, this time, I left the results in God's hands. One day, I decided to look at the community college my neighbor had recommended. I filled out an online application and waited. And waited some more. Finally, on the application deadline date, I called them. The human resources representative said she didn't have copies of my transcripts. I asked her to check again. Suddenly, I remembered that my e-mail address was in my maiden name. I pointed this out to the woman, and she was able to locate my information. She said I would be notified if they were interested. So, I waited once more. Was God trying to teach me patience as well? Finally I received a call for an interview—a month away. I didn't understand. Didn't God know my severance pay would run out before then?

The sight of my dwindling bank account balance prompted me to call my former employer to find out when my last check would arrive and when my health care benefits would end. I was shocked and thrilled to discover I would be getting an additional check for my unused vacation days. What a blessing! In addition, I discovered my vacation time had continued to accrue over the past ten months. As it turned out, I had enough money to take me through another month.

Exactly a year after I was laid off, I started my new job with a salary that was almost identical to my old position. As my feet touched the floor that morning, I praised God for His mercies and for His impeccable timing. And for helping me learn that control is best left to the Master.

—*Connie Hilton Dunn*

Back Home
Again

*Then Jesus said, "Come to me, all of you who are
weary and carry heavy burdens, and I will give
you rest. Take my yoke upon you. Let me teach
you, because I am humble and gentle at heart, and
you will find rest for your souls. For my yoke is
easy to bear, and the burden I give you is light."*

Matthew 11:28–30

The rustle of multicolored leaves danced across
the yard, chased by the breath of a gathering
storm. Summer had lost her battle with the oncoming
tide of winter, her marathon of blooms gone and the
many coats of green replaced by the bleak, monochro-
mic colors. As I gazed out the window, those were the
objects of my thoughts, pushing what should have
been foremost on my mind to the background. Then a

part of my heart—that special compartment reserved for love of family—opened up and released a torrent of emotions.

Sally drifted into the room and kissed my cheek, her breath a whisper against my neck. "I brought you a cup of coffee," she said and handed me the steaming mug. "Care to tell me what's on your mind?"

I took a sip of the strong brew and sighed. "Nothing," I said. Then I saw the reproving look in her eyes. I turned to the window, my forehead pressed against the cool glass, a burst of condensation clouding the windowpane as I spoke. "I don't know. It seems as if everything is coming apart at the seams. I suspect Dad's cancer is far worse than what I'm being told. Mom is still recuperating from her triple bypass surgery. I've been diagnosed with prostate cancer, and I lost my job after thirty-five years. I couldn't have written a drama this tragic on my best day."

I raised my eyes to find a distorted image of Sally and me in the windowpane, our reflections not unlike two ghosts in a horror movie. "Why do we live in this deep freeze?" I asked, in an attempt to change the subject.

"That's a discussion for another day," she said, deftly bringing the subject at hand back to center stage. "Where you need to be right now is West Virginia. Your parents need you, and your sister could use a break. I *know* . . ." she said and held up her hand to stop my protest before continuing. "She claims she doesn't, but that's only to spare you the emotional distress of what is really going on."

Sally was right, of course. I was being a jerk, wallowing in self-pity.

"Give it some thought. I'm sure you'll do the right thing," she said, and left me to my conscience.

Sally's perfume lingered as I reluctantly picked up the phone, the rat-a-tat-tat of hailstones beating a staccato rhythm on the roof as I dialed. "Hello, Mom. I'm coming home."

The bleak November day matched my mood as I left Upstate New York on my way south. Once I crossed the West Virginia border, the layers of winter funk began to peel away, replaced by bright sunshine and a kaleidoscope of colors on the surrounding mountains. As if on cue, John Denver's "Country Roads" drifted through the speakers, and I found myself tapping the steering wheel and singing along, the reason for my trip briefly forgotten.

I passed a little white church, its steeple rising above the crimson leaves of a live oak, and my thoughts drifted back to another time and place, fifty years removed from the present. It was 1954, during a military assignment in Alaska. Two friends and I decided to try our hand at fishing for salmon on the

Russian River, several miles north of Anchorage. We hired a bush pilot to fly us to the mainland, where we borrowed an old limousine for the trip north.

With our gear loaded and our spirits high, we traveled through the Alaskan wilderness, arriving in the early evening and setting up camp a few miles from the river.

The next morning, our fishing gear in tow and our hip waders over our shoulders, we hiked to the river. Little did I know, I was about to have a life-altering experience.

The trees gently swayed to the rhythm of the wind and the sunlight sent sparkles of diamonds dancing across the waves as I waded into the water.

Salmon darted about and leaped from the water like trained dolphins as they made their brutal journey from the ocean to their place of birth. Once there, they would lay and fertilize their eggs, then die—a neverending cycle of life. "I've hooked a big one," I yelled and looked around in hopes of seeing a look of envy on my friends' faces, but they weren't there.

A sudden feeling of foreboding rippled up my spine when the gravel under my feet abruptly gave way. I sucked in my breath as the frigid water enveloped me, my waders immediately filling with water. I struggled to stand, but the current was washing me downstream, my waders pulling me under like an anchor. Then I heard the most awful sound. "A waterfall," I whispered. "My, God, I'm going to die."

There comes a time in most everyone's life when, during a crisis, they turn to God. I was no different. The large boulders, twenty feet below, loomed dark and menacing. The roar of the water was deafening as my frigid hands clung to a log spanning the waterfall. "Dear God," I whispered. "If You get me through this, I promise to spend the rest of my days as a devout Christian." With the prayer still on my lips, I released my grip and plunged into the abyss.

I survived, thanks to a lone angler who witnessed my dilemma, pulled me to safety, and pumped the water from my lungs. I was true to my word. When I returned to my squadron, I found the base chaplain and was baptized the following Sunday.

Now, as I thought back to that time in my life, I suddenly had a desire to visit the little white church. I made a U-turn, the church pulling me like a magnet.

I sat in the parking lot and wondered what had drawn me to this place in the middle of nowhere. An elderly man approached my car and leaned his elbows on the open window. "Name's Harvey. Can I help you?" he said in a familiar West Virginia twang.

"Just thinking," I said, hoping he would go away and leave me in peace.

"You seem put out by something. Sure I can't help?"

"If you must know, I suppose I'm looking for guidance. Spiritual guidance."

"Well, you came to the right place. This here little church has been around since the Civil War. Been a passel of souls saved over the years. Tell you what," he said, as he reached in his pocket and pulled out a small Bible, quickly marking a page with a gnarled finger. "Try this one. It always works for me when I need a little spiritual pick me up."

"Thanks. I'll return your Bible."

"No need. It's yours to keep. The church has plenty of Bibles, but there's only one of you."

"And you are?" I asked.

"Well, right now, I'm what you city folks call a custodian. I do most everything but roof repairs. I don't cotton to roofs. Never did."

As Harvey ambled off, I found the verse and began to read. "Come to me, all of you who are weary and carry heavy burdens, and I will give you rest. Take my yoke upon you. Let me teach you, because I am humble and gentle at heart, and you will find rest for your souls. For my yoke is easy to bear, and the burden I give you is light." As I tried to digest what I had just read, soft music drifted from inside the church. Curious, I entered to find Harvey sitting at the organ. "Welcome," he said. "I'll be with you shortly. And I don't do requests, so don't ask, 'cause I only know three hymns."

"Help me understand, Harvey."

"Well, I can give you a simple country preacher's take on things. Take potholes for example. It takes a leap of faith, not a loss of faith, when you hit one of life's potholes in the road. But if you truly believe, God will help smooth the way. Oh, there will still be potholes, but they won't seem nearly as rough and deep. That's God's promise to you, but only if you honor your promise to Him through faith and prayer."

"I'd like to stay a while and pray. If you don't mind," I said.

"God's church is your church. Stay as long as you like."

"Will you pray with me?"

"It would be my pleasure, son."

So, like the salmon, I was coming home, but not to perish. I was coming home to God, to be born again, and Lord willing, to renew the promises I made all those years ago.

—*Stan Higley*

Blessings in Store

How great is the goodness
you have stored up for those who fear you.
You lavish it on those who come
to you for protection,
blessing them before the watching world.

Psalm 31:19

Our teenage son stood in the driveway and screamed at us. "You hate me," he said. "Why did you bring me here?" I cringed and pressed a hand to my throbbing head as the bitter words spewed from his mouth. "You just love your other precious son. He can get away with anything, but you don't really want me."

What had gone wrong? This son—our sixth child—was supposed to feel loved and wanted. Being a mother should be a woman's greatest blessing, but I didn't know how much more of this I could endure.

When my husband and I married in 1955, we joked about having a dozen children. God took us seriously and, over the next eight years, He blessed us with four delightful daughters and, then, a little boy. We loved children, and God had given us our heart's desire. In the early years of our marriage we lived in town, and our children played with their neighbors. Then we moved to the country. The girls left on the school bus every morning, and our son missed having playmates. By now, we no longer talked about having a dozen children, but we decided half a dozen might be just right. We began to think about adopting a child.

Little did we know that God would continue to fulfill our desire for children, although it wouldn't be in the way we expected. Proverbs 16:9 says, "In his heart a man plans his course, but the Lord determines his steps." In those early days, we had no idea what steps the Lord had in mind for us, or the amount of patience, trust in God, and acceptance those steps would require.

Adoption was a serious commitment, and we prayed for guidance. We were confident we could love an adopted child, so one day I mustered my courage and took the first step. While my husband was at work, I went to the local family services office. I told the caseworker we were interested in a boy about four years old. He and our six-year-old son would have so much fun. I could already visualize them playing on the swings together, building forts, and becoming best friends.

We completed all the paperwork and underwent a home inspection. Then we waited for the phone to ring. There were days when I hardly left the house because I didn't want to miss the crucial call. With pregnancy, we knew the waiting period would be nine months; this time, we didn't know how long it would take. It didn't matter. We would love our new son and raise him to know God. I would mother this little boy just as I did our other children.

A year passed with no word. Then two years, and three, but the call never came. One time, the caseworker said she might have a little boy available, but then she told us it hadn't worked out. After waiting seven years, we decided to give up. Before I got around to letting the caseworker know, she phoned me at the center for developmentally disabled children where I taught. The state had a boy waiting for adoption. Were we still interested? I told her we would think about it. My husband and I read the boy's file and realized adopting this child wouldn't be easy. We put all our trust in God and asked Him to lead us to the right decision.

Allen was thirteen, just eight months younger than our son. The age difference would have been ideal seven years earlier when we first considered adoption, but this child had a troubled history. After much prayer, we decided to meet Allen. We drove across the state for the first meeting, and a few weeks later, we brought him home for a short stay. I arranged for him to visit the local school. He loved everything about the school and our small farm. He was anxious for a permanent home and ready to become part of the family. Soon, we made the final arrangements and brought him home for good.

Our problems started almost immediately. As the new boy in school, Allen wanted the other children to notice him. His attempts to be the cool kid often led to trouble, sometimes of a serious nature. We hoped Allen might feel more secure once the adoption was finalized. After the required waiting period, the three of us went to the courthouse. Allen signed his own adoption papers, and we went to a restaurant to celebrate.

However, legally changing his last name to ours didn't make the problems go away. One of my friends who witnessed our struggles said, "I always thought giving a child love in a Christian home would be enough." But it didn't seem to be enough. As we learned to humble ourselves and submit to those in authority, I wondered if God might be using our experiences with Allen to shape my husband and me.

The school called. Allen had been suspended, and I had to leave my classroom to pick him up. Another time, the sheriff came to our home and took Allen to juvenile detention in handcuffs. My husband and I choked back our tears as we visited strange and disturbing places: juvenile detention hall, group homes, and the county jail. Each place told us when to visit and how long to stay. We didn't agree with all their rules, but we abided by them and came away sobered. The stench of stale cigarette smoke clung to our clothes, a reminder of how far removed we were from our comfort zone.

The caseworker asked if we wanted to reverse the adoption. If she had asked a few years earlier, we might have taken her up on it, but we wouldn't abandon Allen because we believed God was showing us how perseverance comes through the testing of our faith. Allen dropped out of high school, and the day finally came when we had to tell him to leave our home. The juvenile officer advised us to do this to preserve our family. We all needed relief from the constant tension. He was still our son, but he couldn't continue to live with us.

He stayed in the area, married at nineteen, and became a father. Two years later, divorced and alienated from the rest of the community, he left. One February morning, he set off on foot, heading back to his roots on the other side of the state. We had maintained a relationship with his natural grandmother, and we knew he would find his way to her.

There was no dramatic turning point when the struggles ended, and our sixth child became a blessing in our lives. Time and maturity brought about a gradual change in him, and with God's help, we changed, too. We learned to look past the hurt and anger and to love this son who, at times, seemed to hate us. Today, our boy is a grown man and a law-abiding citizen working for a living. He is finally gaining the self-confidence he always needed. After many years of perseverance and heartbreak, we can finally say the blessings outnumber the stormy times. Today, it is a pleasure to answer the phone and hear Allen say, "I just thought I'd call and see what you guys are doing."

—LeAnn Campbell

Tarantulas and
Chocolate Chip Cookies

*I prayed to the Lord, and he answered
me, freeing me from all my fears.*

Psalm 34:4

My husband, Ron, is a family doctor with a heart for missions, so when he was asked to go on a mission trip to the Dominican Republic, he was definitely up for the task. He asked me to join the team, but I'm a fear-filled individual who loves the comfort of my home. I wasn't too responsive, but Ron persisted. On his previous trips, I had always been able to come up with reasonable excuses to avoid going along, but this time, none came to mind. I prayed about it, and to my surprise, I felt compelled to go.

There was one big obstacle standing in my way, however, and that was fear. I was afraid.

Afraid to leave my children behind.

Afraid to travel.

Afraid of contaminated water.

Afraid of sickness.

Afraid of tarantulas.

You name the fear, and I'm sure it made my list. Yet, God was calling me to go, which presented me with a significant problem. During the months leading up to our trip, God graciously reminded me that my fears were not from Him. I had joined a Bible study group, and our topic was Judges. In Judges 6:8, I met a man named Gideon, and, I could relate to him. He and I were kindred spirits—we were both wimps. Yet God saw Gideon as a "mighty hero" (Judges 6:12) and gently proceeded to walk Gideon through his fears. God revealed Himself as Jehovah-Shalom, The Lord Is Peace. And Gideon became the hero God always knew he could be. I began to wonder if, perhaps, God saw me as a mighty hero. Maybe there was hope for me yet.

God continued to bolster my spirit. Our Bible study group talked about a verse from Proverbs 18:10 that said, "The name of the Lord is a strong fortress; the godly run to him and are safe." Hearing this, I decided to take God at His word. I would run to the strong fortress of Jehovah-Shalom and find safety. Being the faithful Father that He is, God did not disappoint. He gently reminded me of His strength and His presence through cards from family, phone conversations with friends, and scriptures He brought to mind. It was amazing to watch Him work. It was exciting to think He had a task for me, His mighty hero. I wasn't going to let Him down!

We arrived on the island of the Dominican Republic safe and sound. We met up with the rest of the group in the airport and proceeded through customs. We spent the night in a hotel in the capital city of Santo Domingo. After a nice dinner buffet and a hot shower, my husband and I hit the sack. *Not too bad for a mission trip. I can handle this!*

The next morning, we began the long, hot journey to San Juan. Our overcrowded, overheated bus almost got the better of me as we bounced and swayed for hours on end. My old fears began to raise their ugly little heads.

Are we going to arrive safely?

What if the bus breaks down?

Am I going to get sick?

Is anyone else going to get sick?

We stopped at a roadside café.

Is this food safe?

What exactly am I eating, anyway?

We finally arrived at the mission in San Juan. My

nerves were frazzled. My stomach was unsettled. My jaw was clenched. The team unpacked the bags, and we got settled into our simple, concrete block rooms. Dinner was served and cleaned up, and preparations were made for the next week. As we worked, the sun began to set, and then nighttime was upon us. As the light faded, the darkness that descended around us simultaneously crept into my spirit. Fear had made itself at home in me, once again.

It was time to get some sleep, so I left the group and headed toward my room. Walking across the compound, I noticed something very large and very hairy resting on the block wall. I knew what it was immediately. The Dominican Republic is known for its oversized tarantulas. I froze. It was then I noticed two men were standing in the courtyard deep in conversation.

"Help?" I whimpered. They didn't seem to hear, so I called out again, this time a little louder. "Help! There's a tarantula over here!"

The two raced to my rescue, maybe a bit more curious than heroic. "Cool! Where is it?"

I pointed to the hairy, circular arachnid on the block wall. "Right there." One of the men, either overly chivalrous or overly ignorant, reached toward the spider. "Don't do that!" I screamed.

"Why not?" he asked. "I don't think you need to be too afraid of this." He picked it up.

"Chocolate chip cookies aren't known to be poisonous," he said as a huge grin appeared on his face.

He handed me a "Chips Ahoy" cookie, and the two had a good laugh at my expense. Feeling utterly ridiculous, I went to my room and got ready for bed.

Our room was simple. It had two twin beds and a stand for our luggage. My husband was already in bed, and I knew it wouldn't be long before he was out for the night. I opened my suitcase and saw something scurry across the wall nearby. Naturally I shrieked at the top of my lungs. Ron laughed and asked why I was so jittery. He told me that having the lizard in our room would keep the insect population at bay.

My heart was thumping and continued to pound as I crawled into my fully inspected bed and turned off the lights. I told Ron I was scared and lonely. Then, I asked if we could move our beds together because I needed him to hold me. No response. When I realized he was wearing earplugs and was nearly asleep, I knew he would be of no use to me whatsoever. What was I going to do?

A full-blown panic attack began to materialize. My heart began racing and my breathing quickened. I started to cry. It was then that I remembered Gideon. I began to pray.

Oh God! This is horrible! I'm scared. I don't know what to do! I'm not going to make it through the night, let alone the entire week like this! Help me! I know you are the God of Peace. You did it for Gideon, please do it for me! God . . . I need your peace. Please deliver me from my fears!

I had no sooner uttered those words than an unbelievable calm came over me. I knew it was from my heavenly Father, and I felt as if His arms were holding me. I slept like a baby that night.

The next morning, I awakened for morning devotions. Our group leader had given all the team members a booklet with predetermined devotions for each day. I opened it and read, Psalm 34:4, the verse for the day. "I prayed to the Lord, and He answered me, freeing me from all my fears." *Oh God! You are so good. You are so intimate and personal. Thank you for hearing my prayers and freeing me from my fears!*

The rest of the week went by in a blur. When I was helping in the pharmacy, cleaning toilets, painting walls, and playing with the schoolchildren, I felt God's peace and presence in a way I never had before. I learned that whether I'm facing tarantulas or chocolate chip cookies, God knows me all too well. He'll meet me right where I'm at—freeing me from fears so I can become His mighty hero!

—LeAnne Blackmore

He Knows
Our Needs

*So don't worry about these things, say-
ing, "What will we eat? What will we drink?
What will we wear?" These things dominate
the thoughts of unbelievers, but your heavenly Father already knows all your needs.*

Matthew 6:31–32

all had come and gone when reality set in. For
the first time in fourteen years, my husband,
Leo, would not be teaching. After much prayer and
soul-searching, we had decided that, because of his
health, he should pursue another line of work. And
yet, whenever I heard the school buzzer off in the
distance calling the students to their classrooms, I
was plagued with misgivings. How soon would Leo
be able to find work? How would we get by with no
regular income in the foreseeable future?

Leo had been a gifted teacher, and I suspected the buzzer tugged at his heart for reasons other than mine. He also was our sole breadwinner and we had financial obligations to meet, especially over the coming winter. We were living in a tiny, poorly insulated cottage that a widow had literally cobbled together with her own two hands during World War II.

At that time, my hometown chamber of commerce was sponsoring a contest with a $50 first prize for anyone who could submit a design for a suitable town crest. Back in the 1950s, $50 went a long way, so while the boys napped, I sat down with scrap paper and pencil and started sketching. When I finally came up with a design that pleased me, I mailed it into the contest, feeling somewhat guilty for squandering money on a stamp.

I often chatted over the back fence with my elderly neighbor lady, and one day, she mentioned that she had smelled wonderful aromas escaping through my open kitchen window. "Would you consider selling some of your home baking?" she asked.

Would I! And then, I hesitated. How could we afford the supplies? Later, I prayed, "Lord, You know all about that contest I've entered. . . ."

The following week, I discovered I had won. A few days later, the phone rang. "This is a local

graphics company calling," the voice on the other end
said. "We understand you are the one who drew the
original design of the town crest. We are very impressed
with your work. Would you be interested in a job?"

I explained quickly that, while I appreciated the
offer, I had no formal training in graphic design. As
I watched our two little boys playing happily on the
floor, I knew I had more important priorities.

When the mail came later that day, I cashed the
$50 check and headed to the grocery store for baking
supplies. I was in business, a mini-business to be sure,
but the seventy-five cents I charged my neighbor for
each pan of cinnamon rolls began to add up. Word
of mouth advertising soon brought in more orders.
People began asking whether I would bake Christmas
cakes as well. Christmas! The very thought of it saddened me. Would I be able to make enough to buy
some modest gifts for the boys and Leo?

In the meantime, I had started to teach Leo how
to type on our old Underwood portable—as much
to take his mind off our situation as to sharpen his
skills. He found it difficult to abandon his "search
and peck" method of typing with two fingers while
staring at the keyboard. I had to constantly remind
him to look up, but when the winter doldrums set in,
I had to take my own advice. Sometimes, it felt as
though God had forgotten us.

Although not conducive to efficient typing, there was one area where Leo's "search and peck" strategy paid off—and that was in his efforts to find a job. He left his name at every employment agency he could find. As a result, he even got a phone call from a modeling agency, offering him exorbitant money for a catalog shoot. When I asked him why he turned it down, I received an indignant reply. "And let everybody I know see me in my underwear? I don't think so!"

When my neighbor arrived to pick up some fresh rolls that week, she asked if I sewed. "I'm not sure if all this home baking is to blame, but I've gained some weight and I need to have a dress altered. Do you suppose you might be able to do it?" That afternoon, she came for a fitting, and I carefully took the measurements of her ample figure and jotted them down. Later, when the boys were in bed, and Leo was scanning the employment ads in the newspaper, I began the alterations. I was not the most experienced seamstress, but as I worked, I prayed that this project would be successful. By the time I went to bed that night, I was confident God had answered my prayer.

The next afternoon when my neighbor came for a fitting, I was absolutely horrified! I had let out every seam possible, and the dress still didn't meet in the middle. Frantic thoughts tore through my head like chain lightning. Had I made an error in my measuring? Was there any way I could rectify my mistake? Would I have to replace the dress? Where would we get the money? "I'm so sorry," I mumbled, my face burning with embarrassment.

"No problem!" my elderly neighbor replied. "I didn't bother to put on my corset today. It'll fit just fine once I get that laced up!" And it did.

I now had a little extra cash to spend on Christmas. Leo's old wristwatch was no longer dependable, but under the circumstances, he felt he didn't really need a new one. After poring over the Eaton mail order catalog, I picked out a couple of toys for each of the boys and an inexpensive watch for Leo.

"But I don't even have a job!" he protested on Christmas morning as he opened his gift.

"It's for when you get one," I replied in a confident voice.

In February, the city called him back. He was given a permanent position in the streets and traffic division, and he began by gathering origin and destination data to expedite traffic flow. The most important requirements for his new job? Minimal typing skills and a reliable wristwatch.

—*Alma Barkman*

Lima Bean
Brownies

*I tell you the truth, anyone who believes in me will
do the same works I have done, and even greater
works, because I am going to be with the Father.*

John 14:12

My husband of five years, Mark, pointed to the platter on the kitchen counter. "What are those green things?" he asked.

"Those are lima bean brownies," I replied in a small voice.

"You've got to be kidding! You don't expect me to eat *those things*, do you?"

My stifled tears spilled over and trickled down my cheeks onto my "Pillsbury Doughboy" apron.

"Did I say something wrong?" he asked.

"Yes . . . I mean . . . no. Oh, I don't know!"

He started to chuckle. "Don't tell me you're crying over lima beans?"

What Mark didn't know, what he couldn't possibly understand is that I had worked all morning, poring over cookbooks and old recipes. I wanted to come up with something creative using the leftover ingredients in the cupboards, which consisted of a canister of flour, a bowl of sugar, a half-empty salt shaker, corn oil, and a can of lima beans. The refrigerator was empty except for two bottles of water, one ice cube tray, and a box of baking soda. That was all that remained of our groceries for the week, a meager supply that had to last us until we left for our overseas assignment in Sicily.

Out of these unlikely ingredients, I had created my pièce de résistance—lima bean brownies! I wiped my stray tears away and explained how I created the new concoction from my mom's favorite brownie recipe by replacing squares of melted chocolate with mashed-up lima beans. As I touted all the benefits of "eating green," Mark shook his head in disbelief. I held up the platter with both hands—as if I had won first place in the "Pillsbury Bake-Off Contest"—and said, "Go on and taste one. They're healthy for you too," I added.

"You're probably right. I'm sure they're very healthy, but you don't really expect me to eat them do you?"

"Of course, I do!"

We had less than two weeks before we left for Sicily, where we would be teaching the Bible for the next six years, and I couldn't muster enough faith to believe that God could provide for our most basic needs. My faith was as dry as the lima bean brownies and as empty as the cupboards. *Where was my trust in God's promises? What good was my Bible school training if I couldn't trust God to provide food for our table?*

As recent Bible College graduates, we were familiar with hard times. For three years, we grew accustomed to eating lentil beans and rice, while we put each other through school. Rolling pennies to pay for laundry and gas was a common occurrence. Yet God had always provided for our needs, and not once did we worry where our next meal would come from. Until now.

With ten days left before our scheduled departure, we had depleted our savings to pay for all of our earthly possessions to be transported to Sicily. Unexpected medical expenses and car repairs had used up our entire budget for the month. For the first time in our life, we had absolutely no money—not even a penny. Mark worked as a summer intern in the youth program at the church we attended, but his paycheck barely covered our monthly expenses, and it wouldn't arrive until the day before we left for Sicily.

Thankfully, we were living rent-free, due to the kindness of friends who allowed us to house sit their summer home in Bradenton, Florida. It was a gated retirement community, flowing with Cadillacs, golf caddies, and swaying palm trees. No one knew that inside the gorgeous three-story condo filled with granite tile and marble floors sat a plate of lima bean brownies that needed to last for a whole week.

Mark held me close while I sobbed. "Remember God's promise?" he whispered.

He pointed to the wall calendar for the month of October. There I read the verse from Matthew 6:25. "That is why I tell you not to worry about everyday life—whether you have enough food and drink, or enough clothes to wear. Isn't life more than food, and your body more than clothing?"

I reached for the calendar and placed it on the refrigerator door. "You're right! We need to trust God for *every*thing." Mark's face beamed with excitement. "C'mon let's eat," he said. "I'm hungry." I took the platter of lima bean brownies and placed them in the center of the table. We clasped hands to pray while Mark offered his customary prayer, "Lord, give us this day our daily bread. . . ." When he finished, I looked up. "Aren't you forgetting something?" I asked.

"Oh, and thank you, Lord, for providing for all of our needs," he added.

I squeezed his hand tightly. "Thanks," I whispered. "I needed to hear that."

As I released his hand, Mark asked politely, "Could you please pass me the main course?"

He had a great way of finding humor, even in the most trying of circumstances. He pretended to cut a slice of prime rib while I tossed the make-believe salad. As I excused myself to get the imaginary salad dressing, the doorbell rang. I called to Mark from the kitchen. "Can you answer that?" I heard the door open. "No one's here, honey," he replied.

"Are you sure? I'm positive I heard the doorbell ring." I joined Mark at the front entrance and glanced down at the steps. A flash of silver glistened in the late afternoon sun. "There's a package on the bottom step!" I said. I scooped up the package, cradled it in my arms as if it was our firstborn, and hurried to the kitchen. There, I carefully laid it on the counter.

Wrapped in two layers of foil was a warm loaf of homemade honey wheat bread—fresh from the oven. I stopped for a moment to savor the sweet aroma. It was heavenly. As I pulled the last layer of foil off the bread, I noticed a snippet of green paper. Mark gave it a gentle tug, and we leaned in to take a closer look. To our surprise, it was a warm and soggy twenty-dollar bill, folded into quarters. Mark carefully unrolled it, wiped the crumbs off with my apron, and held it up to the light. After inspecting it twice, he let out a shout. "It's real! It's a real twenty-dollar bill!"

"Do you believe this?" I asked. "That twenty dollars will see us through until next week."

"God's promises never fail," Mark added. "I think we're going to remember this day for the rest of our lives." I nodded as tears filled my eyes. "Yes, I believe we will."

The following week, we received news that our airline tickets had been paid for, our belongings had arrived safely in Sicily, and the remainder of our support had come in. We would be leaving the United States for Sicily precisely as planned.

It has been twenty-seven years since that simple loaf of bread rested on our doorstep—exactly the miracle I needed to tuck inside my heart and carry with me on the plane to Sicily. God's promise to provide for all of our needs saw us through volcanic eruptions, earthquakes, floods, a cancer diagnosis, and even the loss of loved ones. As we shared the story of how lima bean brownies were transformed into a loaf of bread, God used our blessing to strengthen the faith of others. However, the greatest miracle of all took place in my heart. Now, I know that when I ask for a loaf of bread, God will not give me a "stone" because His promises are *real*.

—Connie Pombo

Is Anyone Here
Mad at God?

So humble yourselves under the mighty
power of God, and at the right time, he will
lift you up in honor. Give all your worries
and cares to God, for he cares about you.

1 Peter 5:6–7

My hand shook as I held the phone. I tried to stand, but I collapsed on the chair as my whole body began to tremble. I had just been told that the diagnosis my husband, Lee, received many years ago was a mistake. "He didn't have Alzheimer's disease," the doctor said.

"Probable Alzheimer's disease" was the original diagnosis we were given on our ninth wedding anniversary. Lee constantly forgot things. His behavior was erratic which meant he couldn't accomplish the work he'd done for more than fifteen years. Eventually, he lost his balance until he was unable to walk at all. He also lost the ability to talk. He couldn't swallow properly or feed himself, and his eyesight deteriorated significantly. After he was admitted to a nursing home, he was diagnosed with a rare brain disease known as progressive supranuclear palsy.

Now, the doctor told me the autopsy revealed that Lee had suffered from viral encephalitis, which had affected the frontal part of his brain. Ultimately, it killed him. "Viral encephalitis can be stopped," the doctor said. "It cannot be reversed, but when diagnosed, it can be stopped."

Suddenly, I felt as if I'd lived with a lie for twenty-two years. Twenty-two years of doing everything possible for Lee. I had accepted my life was changed forever because of his illness, and I gave him the best care I could at home. When I was no longer able to care for him, he went into a nursing facility. Over the years, I shed countless tears over the unrelenting deterioration that took Lee further away from our six children and me.

When he died in June of 2006, my grief was already largely spent, but the results of the autopsy brought additional heartbreak. However, this time, my anguish was accompanied by fierce anger. I was angry with the doctors who had misdiagnosed him. I was angry with God because He allowed it to happen. I was angry with Lee for being sick. I was especially angry with myself because I hadn't asked the doctors the right questions.

The following week at Bible study, I wasn't sure what to share with the others. Ironically—or was it part of God's plan—the study focused on anger toward God. At the end of the lesson, our leader had a question for the group. "Is anyone here mad at God?"

As if possessed with a life of its own, my arm rose, and I began to cry. At first, I was too overwhelmed to speak. Finally, I told them. "My husband was misdiagnosed. He didn't have to suffer all those years. He didn't have to leave me and die."

"Does God care?" the study leader asked. "Is He still in control? Can God use what happened for His glory? Can He honor you for your years of loving devotion to your husband?" Later, we all prayed, and I left that night feeling better—for a while.

I couldn't stop thinking about the things I had missed. No more Saturdays searching for bells to add to our collection, no Bible studies together, no nights of sharing our intimate thoughts, and no family vacations. I had learned to live with all these things after the doctors told me my husband had an incurable disease. The anger returned. I thought about suing the doctors, but I knew it wouldn't bring back Lee or the years we'd missed.

During Lee's illness, I had studied the book of Job. Now, I opened my Bible for another look. Job didn't deserve the tragedies that occurred. Even though he didn't understand why everything happened, he accepted his losses as God's will. As I prayed and turned my anger over to God, I began to see how He had used me during my years as Lee's caregiver.

Right after Lee went on disability retirement, I asked God how I could supplement the disability income. He had one word for me: "Write." I became serious about writing for publication, which led to occasional speaking engagements. This was a remarkable development since I've always been shy, and I had grown up thinking I wasn't capable of doing anything. According to my parents, "After all, you're just a girl."

Lee had believed otherwise. He pushed me to write, become PTA president, teach a junior high Sunday school class, and share the history of our antique bell collection with various groups. He sustained me with endless encouragement, and during our family devotions, he would remind me that my power came from God—not from him and not from my parents. "God loves you, Marcia," he said. "He will give you the power to succeed in what He wants for your life—including your writing."

Thanks to Lee's guidance and support, I was able to accept an invitation to be a part of an advocacy committee, despite my fears. The committee worked to pass three bills that would help the families of people under the age of sixty-five who suffered from Alzheimer's disease or a related disorder. Lee had been forty-one when he went on disability retirement. For months, I spoke to various committees at the Oregon State Legislature about the needs of families like mine.

Invariably, I would shake as I spoke, and I often left the meeting with a migraine, but I still managed to inform people of the unusual needs of young families with a disabled parent. Because of this incredible opportunity, three bills passed. One was designated to start an Alzheimer's research center in Portland, the second was to fund this center, and the third provided in-home help for families with a disabled parent under the age of sixty-five through Oregon Project Independence.

Since Lee's death, I've continued to write and to speak. I believe the Lord has used my writing and speaking to help others, but He has also used these things to help me cope during the countless changes that occurred over twenty-two years. I may never fully comprehend why God allowed Lee's illness and early death, but now I know it was part of His perfect plan—for His own good reason.

—*Marcia Alice Mitchell*

Blue Roses

I have swept away your sins like a cloud.
I have scattered your offenses
like the morning mist.
Oh, return to me,
for I have paid the price to set you free.

Isaiah 44:22

The posh department store glittered around me. Shopping bag in hand, I hugged my purse, guarding the $25 I'd earned. Spring sweaters glowed on the racks. Gold pendants slid through my outstretched hand. One aisle over, my partner-in-crime winked, then slipped a silk scarf into her purse. No alarm rang overhead. No bolt of lightning struck. She lifted one brow—a double-dog dare.

I took a deep breath and edged along the jewelry counter. I'd already stashed two belts in my bag while in the dressing room. Now, I spotted a pair of earrings embellished with blue roses. Abruptly, I thought of my ex-boyfriend, Ben. He had introduced me to Tennessee Williams's *The Glass Menagerie*, a heartbreaking play about abandonment. The earrings slid out of focus as scene two replayed in my mind. The former high school hero, now an adult, recalls asking Laura why she'd missed class.

"Pleurosis," she said, not meeting his eyes.

Ben had heard "blue roses" instead. He grinned and began calling Laura by that name. No common weed, the girl seemed rare and wondrous, a new species. Had Ben ever seen me that way? Had anyone?

I slipped an earring free and held it against my ear, stroking the small rose. Ben had recently told me to grow up. "Trust God," he said, "and show some respect for your parents. Accept the divorce."

Anger rose again. A furtive look, and then I slipped the back off the second earring. But the top-heavy post struck the glass counter with a clatter. Startled, I backed away, but not fast enough.

A hand cinched my bicep and squeezed, propelling me forward. "This way, kid. No funny business. Your friend can wait." Low and hoarse, the voice broke up in a harsh cough. I risked a glance. Over-bleached hair framed a face with bad skin, thin lips, and an overbite.

Poised to sprint, my friend molded herself to a rack nearby, stolen loot stuffed behind her. *My first heist and I'm busted,* I thought. Served me right. I was the daughter of a lawyer and granddaughter of a judge. I had no excuse. We not only upheld the law, we *were* the law. The way I was brought up; Dad was practically God.

But, as my shopping pal had earlier confided, Dad had broken the sixth commandment. "A big 'A' for adultery," she said. Sure enough, he abandoned us and remarried. Feeling betrayed and bewildered, I conspired to hurt him back. I questioned everything after that, especially God. Feeling ignored by heaven, I rebelled.

Now, the store detective's grip hustled me into a yellow makeshift office. When she frisked me, I stared at her upper lip. She'd have a mustache soon. As if sensing my revulsion, she sat me down hard, in a folding chair. It was just the two of us in a room overcrowded by the presence of my guilt. My absent father's disdain registered in every cell of my body, along with Grandpa's ghost, sitting in judgment.

"Driver's license?" Dread rolled through my stomach as I dug for my wallet. Surely she knew the family name. "Purse on the desk," she added. "And the bag." She picked up the phone and dialed a number, then rifled through the sack, checking the contents against my receipts. I had bought socks and shampoo to get a stash bag. "What about these?" She held up the belts. I looked away.

"You're lucky. If you'd taken the earrings, too, you'd be charged with a felony." She laughed. "You sure jumped when that second one fell."

Outside a siren wailed. Within moments, the office door opened and the beefiest cop in the world filled the doorframe, one hand on his holster. "Let's go," he said.

They each seized one of my arms, parading me past cosmetics, accessories, shoes, then out the double glass doors to the squad car, its red and blue lights flashing. Customers stared. My friend slunk into her car, to follow us. The cop's hand lowered my head, just like on TV, and I crumpled into the back seat, behind the grille. Up the scale and down again that siren wailed for what seemed like forever.

Click. Flash. Repeat. Down at the station, mug shots made me blink back stars. "Prints next," another policeman said. *Dad's going to disown me. Grandpa's bones must be rattling in his coffin.* Big hands mashed my right thumb into black ink on a slab, and then pressed it to a page. My fingertips were next, done in a slow, rolling motion. God-given and unrepeatable, the crisp whorls and ridges reproached me.

I swallowed tears as the captain strode toward me with a glower on his face. "Big mistake, young lady," he said. "This goes on your record. Future employers will check your applications." More dire pronouncements followed, and two other policemen joined in. There was no need to scare me. My spirit was molten. *I'm a fool—all for two belts. And those tattletale blue-rose earrings.* I apologized over and over, but they weren't done yet.

"Your fine is $25," the captain said. "Payable now. Or you don't leave."

I nodded dumbly, counted out tens and ones from my wallet. It never occurred to me to call anyone. I'd pay the fine and settle things. No one need know. I said little to my partner-in-crime as we drove home, and even less to my family at dinner that night. Maybe, just maybe, they wouldn't find out. But it haunted me.

Within days our local paper published the facts. I was slouched on Grandma's hide-a-bed when Dad came in and shook *The Enterprise* in my face. At such close range, his teeth seemed longer. A few missed whiskers bristled. Among other things, he said, "I don't know how I'm going to keep this from your grandmother. It'll probably kill her. I'm glad my father's not alive to see this."

Gram's mantel clock ticked relentlessly. My head weighed too much for my aching neck. Backbone, ego—I felt myself bowing over, a seedling in a down-pour. The parent who used to "cloud up and rain all over me" let fly with a tempest that day, slapping the paper, the mantel, pacing the carpet. Finally, he ran a hand through his graying hair. "Why didn't you come to me for help?"

I straightened. Had I heard right? He hadn't called for months, hadn't visited, hadn't invited me over. Yet, his shadow was omnipresent. Never there in the flesh, now he wanted to help me? His look was intense, almost pleading. "Why?" he repeated.

I tugged at a raveled place on the hide-a-bed. "You said if I ever got in trouble, I was on my own."

His intake of breath was sharp, as though a lance had pierced his lung. He bent his head in silence.

"I had the money, so I paid." It was cash he had given me for a painting I did for his office, so technically, *he* had paid the price for my crime. Still resenting his sudden reversal, I didn't tell him that. Why should he have the satisfaction of thinking he'd rescued me? Still, I never could resist a chance for his approval. Guilt tightened its noose. "Dad, wait. I'm sorry. It was stupid."

"Getting caught? Or stealing?"

This wasn't his usual sarcasm—he wanted to know. Did he really think so little of me? No wonder

he had left us. Turning, I mumbled, "I'll tell Gram."
A kind of penance. Maybe if I groveled enough.

"No." His big-knuckled hand halted me mid-step.
"I'll cover for you. Leave her to me. Don't worry
about what anyone else says, either. You've learned a
hard lesson. These things happen."

He was *defending* me. Blue roses could have burst
from his fingertips and I wouldn't have been more
surprised. My breath caught in my throat. "You mean
it?" I felt younger, lighter, and completely cleansed.
His compassion at that moment reminded me of
God's mercy: potent, unearned, and inexplicable.

Dad pushed his glasses up his nose self-consciously.
"Just don't do it again. And keep coming over, okay? I
like having you around." The Law had spoken, and
what I heard was grace.

—*Laurie Klein*

A Valuable
Lesson

*Instead, invite the poor, the crippled, the
lame, and the blind. Then at the resurrection of the righteous, God will reward you for
inviting those who could not repay you.*

Luke 14:13–14

Mary Ann's brow wrinkled as she strained to
see the tiny beads. "I'm almost done with my
brooch," she said. "Sometimes I feel like it will never be
finished. I can't even do a simple thing like threading a
needle anymore." Desperation showed in her eyes as she
struggled with the thread. She threw up her hands in
surrender and looked at me hopefully. "Would you finish it for me?" she asked in a timid voice. She handed
me the kit I had given her to work on a week earlier.

I pasted a smile on my face. "No problem," I replied.
"I'll be glad to put the beads around the edge." Trying to look pleasant was difficult when my mind was

churning out complaints. *The teacher shouldn't be doing the projects for the students. I should have told her I'd take it home and finish it later. I don't have time for this.*

Until that day I thought helping the poor, the crippled, and the blind meant dishing up food for the homeless at the rescue mission and giving used clothing to charity. Not spending hours working on a bead project for someone else when there were tons of other things I'd rather be doing for myself. I'm embarrassed to recall my thoughts as I completed Mary Ann's brooch. Even though it took only two hours, those two hours had been filled with self-centered, prideful thoughts of how I was wasting my time by working on projects unworthy of my skill.

Our needle arts class consisted of twelve women, each working on a beaded brooch. Some completed theirs during the week, but Mary Ann was still working on hers at our next meeting. She was a diabetic, and I suspected that part of the reason she didn't finish was her failing eyesight. There were other things that prevented her from spending time on her brooch. She ran a home care facility for the aged, spent hours working on showers for brides-to-be and new mothers, and decorated cakes. She referred to her work as a "labor of love." Her limited budget didn't stop her from blessing others with lovely gifts such as hand-knitted Afghans and baby sweaters.

She was obviously thrilled when I returned her completed brooch. "Oh, thank you Midge," she said. "It's beautiful." Her brilliant smile made me feel guilty for my attitude, and I hoped she hadn't noticed my earlier reluctance.

On Easter Sunday, I joined Mary Ann as she sat in the foyer waiting for church to begin. While we visited, she glanced often at the brooch, displayed with pride on her jacket. "Thanks again for finishing the pin for me," she said. "It feels so good to have a project completed." Three days later it was time for our class. "Is Mary Ann coming?" Sue asked.

I glanced at my watch. "She called last night to assure me she would be here," I replied.

The church secretary appeared in the open door of our meeting room. "Midge, you have a phone call," she said.

Who would call me here? I picked up the receiver.

Mary Ann's assistant was on the line. "Midge, this is Margaret. I don't know how else to tell you this, but Mary Ann died early this morning. I called because I remembered she had planned on coming to your meeting this morning, and I didn't want you waiting and wondering about her."

I searched for words to break the stunned silence. "I'm so sorry, Margaret. Is there anything I can do?"

"I don't know," Margaret said, "Mary Ann didn't have any living relatives. The church and your sewing group were her family. Her patients have already been taken to other care facilities." Margaret's words were punctuated by sobs.

"I'll stop by on my way home," I said.

As I replaced the receiver, I thought about the last time I had seen Mary Ann. She had been smiling and looking at her brooch. What if I hadn't taken the time to help her finish it? No doubt, I would have hurt her feelings and disappointed her, but I also would have suffered the consequences of my selfish action and missed out on a huge blessing. Thankfully, I didn't have to endure the guilt of knowing I had missed the opportunity to perform an act of kindness, but the thought that I did it with a less than enthusiastic attitude troubled me.

Later, I remembered a time when I couldn't stitch anything. A teacher noticed me struggling with a beginning project. "Can I help you?" she asked.

"I don't think so," I said, "I'm not going to be able to finish this. My shoulder hurts because of a bursitis attack, and my stitch count is totally off. I see myself tearing out a lot of stitches in my future."

The teacher smiled and took the piece out of my hands. "If you don't mind, I'll take it home, fix it and bring it back next time."

She brought the finished piece to the next class. It was gorgeous, and I was ecstatic. She had spent hours taking out my mistakes and then many more hours finishing it. How had I forgotten such a great act of kindness?

That afternoon I walked around Mary Ann's home, surrounded by the evidence of her many of acts of kindness. There were pictures of the children who had been her charges when she was a nanny. Anyone who knew her also knew those children were as precious to her as if they were her own. Unfinished Christmas presents for friends sat beside a card thanking her for baking a cake for a baby shower.

That's when I understood that following God's command to help the needy didn't just mean providing meals for the homeless or donating clothes to the poor. It meant sharing the gifts with which the Lord has blessed me, not hoarding them for my own benefit. My realization helped me learn to share with others and to look for opportunities to help. I thought I was doing Mary Ann a favor the day I helped her with her brooch. I had no idea that she was the one teaching me a valuable lesson.

—*Midge DeSart*

Vision in
a Verse

But those who trust in the Lord will find new strength.
They will soar high on wings like eagles.
They will run and not grow weary.
They will walk and not faint.

Isaiah 40:31

"Honey, I need a bit of money." My husband looked up from the book on his desk, and I continued. "I went to the Christian bookstore today, and just before I left, I found a banner with Isaiah 40:31 on it. I know that's my verse for the year." I took a deep breath and waited for a response. He didn't answer, so I prompted his memory. "Remember when my friend Vonnie suggested I find my Bible verse for the year?" I asked. "Well I think I've found one!"

"How much do you need?"

I shrugged. "No clue. It's a big banner." I spread my hands about two feet apart. I felt like one of our teenagers pleading for the latest electronic gadget. "All I know is I've searched my Bible and prayed to find this verse. I didn't have any money with me, but I thought if I browsed the store I'd find something. When I got back to car, I realized God had placed that verse right in front of me. I really, really felt Him talking to me."

I knew I didn't need to explain any further, but I wanted to rush back to the store before they sold the wonderful banner. My words tumbled over themselves as I tried to convince Gary how much I needed it. He's a preacher, and as far as he's concerned, if you have the words in your Bible and you scribble them on paper, that's enough. I'm different; I need visuals.

Gary pulled out his wallet. "I've only got a twenty. If it's more, you might need to make your own banner," he said with a smile. I kissed him and hurried from his study.

At the store I searched for the huge banner, but I couldn't find it. I finally asked a clerk. "Did you sell a large banner?" I asked and then described it, but she told me they hadn't sold any banners that afternoon.

"The only item like the one you're describing are these parchments," she said and led me to some four-by-six-inch scrolls that sold for $1.79.

The first one had Isaiah 40:31 printed on it. "But those who trust in the Lord will find new strength. They will soar high on wings like eagles. They will run and not grow weary. They will walk and not faint."

Surprised by how large the banner had seemed in my mind, I purchased the tiny scroll and returned the change to Gary. He didn't tease me about my "huge banner" then or later.

In the days that followed, my verse proved its value. When someone in our church became disgruntled with me, I felt the excitement begin to drain from my spiritual life. The nights were endless and filled with anxiety, but when I couldn't sleep, I focused on my verse. When the unhappy parishioner wrote a letter about me to the district superintendent, I felt deeply wounded. The superintendent suggested I give up my other positions in the church and content myself with being the preacher's wife.

I cried. I didn't want to step down. My inner spirit said, "Stand up and fight," but I followed the superintendent's advice. God had known what I needed before any problems arose. I found solace, hope, and strength in Isaiah and stepped aside to allow my husband to work out church problems.

Armed by the results of the first year, I claimed a new verse—Psalm 27:1—in December. "The Lord is my light and my salvation—so why should I be afraid? The Lord is my fortress protecting me from danger, so why should I tremble?" Nine months later, I found a lump in my left breast. The fear of cancer was overwhelming, but my verse reminded me that God was aware of my problems long before I discovered them. His promise of hope gave me strength while we waited for the test results. "Mrs. Crawford, I have good news. The lump was benign."

Twenty years later, I woke up at four on a stormy December morning to begin the search for my yearly verse. I had been looking for weeks. That morning, I flipped page after page in my Bible to review my comments, sermon notes, and the explanatory remarks at the bottom of each page. "You look pretty studious for this time of day." Gary's voice surprised me. He rarely got up at the crack of dawn.

"I can't find my Bible verse for next year." I watched him wander to the kitchen for coffee. When he returned, I waited for him to comment on my search, but he said nothing. "Can I assume your silence means you think I'm wasting my time?" I asked.

"It might not be my way, but that doesn't mean I believe it's a waste of time." He took a sip of his coffee. "This is your spiritual journey."

Although Gary had retired from the ministry, his words that day felt like one of his sermons. He was right. Not everyone chooses a verse for the year. I had often encouraged him to find a verse with me. I would tell him all the ways God had blessed me with my scripture memorization, but now I understood. It wasn't for everyone.

Over the years, I had shared my verse habit with Sunday school classes, women's ministries groups, and our children. Only a few people had followed my lead, but in the quiet of that morning while Gary drank coffee, I settled on Psalm 150—six verses devoted entirely to praising God. "I'm not sure why I feel led to use a whole chapter," I said. "Maybe the Lord wants me to memorize more?" I had no idea that in only a few days an ophthalmologist would send me to an eye specialist.

"We have bad news and good news, Mrs. Crawford," the doctor said. "You have Fuch's Dystrophy and, at present, you're legally blind." He told me a cornea transplant would enable me see again. "We'll place your name on a donor list and perform a cornea transplant. After a year, we'll remove the stitches and you will be able to see again."

He made it sound simple. It wasn't.

With his announcement, I lost my independence. I was no longer allowed to drive, and my world became a little box with no way out. In desperation, I started creating memory books for our children and grandchildren. In the event I lost my sight, I wanted them to have photos and facts about our family heritage. Every day, I left our kitchen and enclosed front porch in a chaotic mess of cropped pictures, chopped up cards, and memories. In the middle of the night, I'd wake up in a panic and mumble my praises until I fell asleep. In the daytime I memorized Psalm 150. If I focused on praise, fear stayed away.

Then in August the phone call came. "Mrs. Crawford, you are scheduled for surgery tomorrow."

I walked into the surgical center behind a courier with a plastic ice chest. As he signed a form at the desk, the receptionist smiled at me. "This package is for you," she said. "It's your new cornea."

I closed my eyes in silent prayer. *Oh, Lord, You knew in December that someone would die that I might see. Father, I praise You for my sight. I ask You to give Your peace to the donor's family.*

Nine years later, I underwent a second transplant. I have good vision in both eyes, and years of choosing a scripture on which to focus has cleared my spiritual vision as well. Year after year, God has given me new insight through His eternal vision in a verse.

—*Katherine J. Crawford*

Satisfaction
Guaranteed

Don't love money; be satisfied with what you have. For God has said, "I will never fail you. I will never abandon you." So we can say with confidence, "The Lord is my helper, so I will have no fear. What can mere people do to me?"

Hebrews 13:5–6

It was the phone call I had been dreading. A strange woman asked for me by name, but when I responded, there was a moment of silence before she continued. "I'm sorry to tell you this."

"Yes?" I sat down on the edge of a chair, the telephone's receiver pressed close to my ear.

"Your son walked out of the program this afternoon. Remember, since he isn't a minor, we couldn't detain him."

"Thank you for letting me know." My heart hurt. I stood up, the silent telephone receiver in my hand, and stared out the window. Just two days before, our son, Dave, had flown to Hawaii where he had agreed to check into an alcohol treatment program. He traveled on a one-way ticket and per the center's strict policy, he took a little clothing, a telephone calling card, and a few dollars.

I had just arrived home from work when I got the call. I wondered what Dave would do. He was familiar with the island. Two years earlier, he'd lived in Honolulu for about six months. Maybe he'd look up old friends, get a job, and stay.

Dave was a new teen when we discovered he had been drinking alcohol with his friends. Our efforts to help him only seemed to make matters worse. He continued to find a way to get alcohol, openly rebelled, and often skipped school. It wasn't long before he developed a serious drinking problem.

One day, I got a call that he had walked out of class again and left the grounds, which wasn't allowed at the private school he attended. Determined to find him, I got permission to leave work early and started looking for him. When I spotted him, he was walking into a store parking lot, his skateboard under his arm, surrounded by a group of boys. I drove up, as close as I dared, and called out. "Dave. Come here. I need to talk to you."

"Leave me alone," he shouted. He glared at me, his anger obvious, and his words slurred. "I don't want to talk to you. Get out of here." He turned and walked away.

I drove away in tears. Soon, our son abandoned our family and moved in with a friend. The following weeks brought more anguish and no answers, but as I prayed for guidance, my trust in God remained firm.

One day at work, a coworker shared some good news. "Charlotte, I got a promotion. There's one more position open. Go for it. You'd get a nice raise, too."

Applying for a promotion wasn't on my mind. Finding a way to reach my son was the only thing I could think about. "I've already turned in my notice," I said. "I've decided to work in our church office. I've been hired as the new secretary."

"Are you crazy?" My friend shook her head as she flipped through the papers on her desk. "Why would you give up your state job to work as a church secretary? It doesn't make any sense. I know it won't pay you what you make here. And what about promotional opportunities?"

For me, the answer was clear. I had to trust God. It wasn't about the money or promotions. From the first day of my new job, I knew I'd made the right decision. I was able to take off all the time I needed to help Dave. Many times after school, I'd get off work early, so we could talk. Sometimes, we'd go for a drive.

Eventually, he began to open up and talk. During our times together, he cried and spoke from his heart. Finally, he returned home and became the loving son I'd known. But his life was still full of ups and downs as he struggled with his alcohol problem.

When he left for the treatment center on the North Shore of Hawaii, we could only pray that he would stay and accept the help he needed. The telephone call told me he was still rebellious, a sign of his dissatisfaction with his life.

He phoned that evening. "Mom, I couldn't stay there." He paused. "I used my last dollar to ride the bus to the city. I need to come home. Please buy me a plane ticket."

I didn't answer.

He talked fast. "You'll get me a ticket, right? I'll call back tomorrow," he said and hung up.

I went to work the next day, my mind in a whirl. I wanted to rush to the nearest travel agency and arrange a flight home for Dave, but I couldn't. I didn't have enough money, and I didn't feel it would be a wise decision.

Around noon he called. "Mom, did you buy it?"

"No, not yet."

"Why not? What's wrong? Do you hate me or something?" He was silent for a few seconds, and then he continued, his voice rising. "I'm hungry. I'm tired. Are you going to leave me here alone to die?"

"No. It's just that we don't have the money. I . . . ."

He interrupted, his voice loud and shrill. "Well, borrow it. What's the deal? Do you love me or not?" He began to sob.

"You know we love you. It's not about the money. Or a plane ticket."

He hung up. Moments later, he called back. "Mom, don't you get it? I'll have to sleep on the beach and start eating out of garbage cans."

"You have friends over there. Can't you stay with one of them? Just until we can figure out what to do?"

He hung up, but he continued to call several times a day for the next few days. He'd always argue with whatever I said and then, hang up on me. Eventually his calling card ran out, and I had no number to call him back. For the next few days, I struggled through the hours, praying and wondering where he was and how he was surviving.

Early on the following Saturday morning, our phone rang. "Mom, I'm in Seattle. It's an unbelievable story. There's a long layover for the plane to Portland so I bought a bus ticket. I'll call when I get there." He hesitated, "Is it okay? If I come home?"

"Of course," I said. "You know you're always welcome to come home." Around noon, I met him at the bus station. We hugged in silence, tears in our eyes.

Today, Dave is quick to tell others how the homeless experience changed his life, and how his eyes were opened to the value of his life and the lives of those he loved. He also relates that even though he'd felt abandoned on the shores of Hawaii, he knew God would never leave him.

Dave has been free of his alcohol addiction for more than six years. Of course, things aren't always easy, but he's learned to be satisfied with what he has. He's happy, healthy, and a vital part of our close-knit family. I've since returned to a promotional position with the state. Both Dave and I can confidently assure others that God will never fail or abandon them. He was, and always will be, our greatest helper.

—*Charlotte Kardokus*

Journey to Joy

The young women will dance for joy,
And the men—old and young—
will join in the celebration.
I will turn their mourning into joy.
I will comfort them and exchange
their sorrow for rejoicing.

Jeremiah 31:13

I glared at Sheila and Steven. "No," I said. "Absolutely not!" *And mind your own business*, I thought.

Sheila smiled, and Steven, ignoring my folded arms, continued. "It's obvious God brought you and Gus together," he said. "We're going to keep praying." Sheila and Steven were faithful friends, and while I was old enough to be Sheila's mother, I worked part-time at her bookstore. Being disrespectful is not my nature, but I probably slammed the office door and stormed out. I intended to run my own life without advice, and I would not get married again. Never. Not me!

As a grandmother heading up our three-member, three-generation household, challenges greeted me every day, but I prayed a lot, life was good, and we were safe.

It hadn't always been that way. Many years before, when my children's father and I divorced, I threw God out of my life and set out to "make it on my own." What I did was to make a big mess of my life.

Although I was smart enough to run a successful small business, I had found myself in an unhealthy and abusive marriage that brought additional hard times. After my daughter's baby was born, her own marriage failed. My sweet Melinda, who struggled with disabilities, eventually came home for refuge. Survival became more difficult, and my soul was dry. The controlling man I married had allowed no religious activity of any kind, I had cut myself off from family and friends, my Marine Corps son was a zillion miles away in the Persian Gulf War, and I was afraid.

Finally, after years of being trapped in a corner, I fell on my face before the God of my youth even though I didn't think He would remember me or care. I had forgotten He was a forgiving God who worked in mysterious ways.

I continued to pray and came to the conclusion that I must leave my marriage. Plans gelled, and I began "stealing" my own money. But where to hide it? Aha! My husband never touched my Bible. So, late at night, as I stashed my money, my eyes fell on first one Bible verse and then another. Many nights, as my husband slept off another drunk night, I spent hours, engrossed once more, in God's sweet word. Claiming one promise after another, I cried out for forgiveness and the meaning of the cross became real to me again.

God helped me repair broken relationships with my family, and His promises gave me courage to start a new life. He gently guided Melinda, five-year-old John, and me to safety. Things did not change overnight, and the journey was never easy. Bright sunshine often collided with dark, frightening days, but I stumbled on, through setbacks and roadblocks. I had experienced God's restoration and faithfulness, and I did not look back. Instead, I dug deeper into His word, and as life improved, I vowed to stay blissfully single for the rest of my life.

In due course, we settled in a small community in the Texas hill country, the place where our true healing began. We found a church that made us feel at home, made good friends, and stayed in touch with my extended family. My job as director of a senior citizen's activity center brought such delight to my heart that it seemed God's promise to me from Jeremiah 31:13 had been fulfilled. The women in the line dancing classes were young at heart and danced for joy, while the older men celebrated events like necktie contests on Father's Day.

The years passed quickly. John hit adolescence, and I retired from the senior center, taking a part-time job so Melinda and I would have more freedom to enjoy John's activities. I loved my work at Sheila's Christian bookstore and our home echoed with teenagers' laughter.

One weekend, I attended the 103rd birthday party for a lovely lady in our community. The celebration of Anna's beautiful life was charming and later, her oldest son, a widower and a gentleman in every way, invited me to dinner. Gus was a man of deep faith. We had much in common, and both longed for conversation with an adult of our own generation. I refused any kind of serious relationship, and as a new widower, Gus was comfortable with my decision. Occasionally he invited me to a family dinner or participated in a gathering at my home. A sweet friendship developed over the next year.

All was well until the day in the bookstore when my employer's husband suggested that Gus would make a fine husband for me. I immediately broke off my friendship with Gus. He was not happy, but I stood firm.

My grandson said, "Grandma, you were a lot happier when you and Mr. Gus went out now and then."

I responded in a sharp, determined tone. "I'm perfectly happy—just tired. Do your homework."

I immersed myself even further in John's school events and in Bible study classes. Months later, word came that Gus's mother had died just after her 104th birthday. With a heavy heart, I respectfully called on the family. Gus was pleased to see me, and I joined the family in mourning as we laid sweet Anna to rest.

Then, while the crisp days of fall colored our hills, my steadfast resolve began to crumble. A year later, Gus and I married. His children and my children gathered with us at our marriage altar to ask God's blessings on our union. My daughter and grandson moved with me to Gus's farm, and our hearts and households blended so easily that once again, God overcompensated in keeping His promise to turn my mourning into joy.

As it turned out, He wasn't finished.

Close to our sixth anniversary, all twenty-nine of our combined children, grandchildren, great-grandchildren, spouses, and special-intendeds gathered to celebrate Gus' eighty-fifth birthday. Our own siblings and families, miscellaneous other relatives, neighbors, and a passel of friends—including Sheila and Steven—were also present. The party swirled about me as I stood on the back porch of our home.

"Granddad, come cut your cake."

"Great party, Liz!"

"Love your lemonade."

I hugged our children, friends, and neighbors, while some of the young adult grandkids waved as they returned from showing their friends around the old farm. Younger grandchildren hollered at me from limbs of the tree Gus had climbed as a boy, and great-grandchildren danced around my legs. Joy and laughter enveloped me. I wiped away tears of joy, and Gus winked at me over the heads of our guests.

Young women danced for joy across our lawn. Men—his family and mine, old and young—joined in the celebration. Our mourning had turned into deep, abiding joy in each other and in our Lord. We were comforted. God had exchanged our sorrow for rejoicing.

—*Liz Hoyt Eberle*

An Eye
for Detail

*Work willingly at whatever you do, as though
you were working for the Lord rather than
for people. Remember that the Lord will
give you an inheritance as your reward, and
that the Master you are serving is Christ.*

Colossians 3:23–24

Following a phone interview, my husband Rick and I flew from Illinois to Florida for a face-to-face interview. We arrived on Friday and drove a borrowed car to the small barrier island. I stared at the Australian pines and palm trees lining the causeway and marveled at the picture postcard azure waters as we drove over the bridge. *Could this ever be familiar?*

We found ourselves in front of a small, wood-framed church. Tropical scents wafted on the salty air. Rick tested the door to the church, and much to our surprise, it opened. We stepped inside the seventy-six-year-old building. Varnished, arched frames housed windows that no longer opened; it was like walking into the past. Oppressive heat magnified the musty odor. Faded green carpet covered hardwood floors in the aisles between wooden theater chairs bolted to the floor.

I wiped a trickle of perspiration from my face. "Go stand behind the pulpit," I said.

Rick stepped onto the small platform and leaned on the pulpit while lifting one arm in a mock-lecture pose. The following day, I sat on one of those hard chairs among the gathering crowd. Air conditioning fought the sunlight filtering into the church through frosted windowpanes. The church held about 120, and half the seats were filled with unfamiliar faces. For years, I had prayed for my husband's ministry. I watched people flourish and grow spiritually under his teaching at our in-home Bible studies. Now, it looked like the answer to my prayers would take me away from the place I had lived all my life—away from family, friends, and the church God had used to turn my life around.

We left behind financial security, medical benefits, and our own home to accept the small church's offer: $200 a week, housing in the parsonage, and promised increases as the church grew. For three years, we supplemented our income with money we had made from the sale of our home. The church's membership increased, and when our savings ran out, we approached the deacons.

"We need another $50 a week to make our bills," Rick said. The head deacon said they would discuss it.

Rick met with the deacons, and I prayed. Hours later, Rick walked in the door wearing a disheartened expression.

"What happened?"

"They want proof."

"Proof? Proof of what?"

He slumped onto one of the dining room chairs. "They want copies of our bills. Proof we really need the money."

The lack of trust stunned me, but even more, it hurt. We made the requested copies, and the deacon board offered to increase Rick's pay by $25—not the $50 we needed. I didn't know what to think. Rick had given up so much and worked so hard. The board's actions angered me.

"God is the one who brought us here," Rick reminded me. "We are here to serve Him, and somehow He will take care of our needs." He took my hand. "'Work hard and cheerfully at whatever you do, as though you were working for the Lord rather than for people. Remember that the Lord will give you an inheritance as your reward, and the Master you are serving is Christ.'" I recognized the familiar verse, but Rick's face mirrored my own struggle to accept it at this moment.

We went on with God's work, trusting him. I had my ups and downs. That week at the ladies' Bible study I broke into tears. "What's wrong?" the woman across the table asked.

I didn't like to talk about money because I didn't want people to think I was trying to manipulate them into helping us. I struggled for a few minutes to find the balance between trusting God and making a need known. I explained the financial dilemma and answered questions. Most of the people there didn't realize that almost a third of our pay went to self-employment taxes. Nor did they know we had been living on our savings.

The growing church brought new responsibilities, and we still grappled to make ends meet. We didn't mind giving of our time and money, or even having only one day off a week, but living next to the church took its toll. Instead of ministry, the role of pastor became a 24/7 job, and we lived at work. With no money, I realized I'd probably live in the parsonage until we retired, but then what? Rick expressed the same concern. If something should happen to him, where would I live? We made it a matter of prayer, but I silently resigned myself to never owning a home again.

Small gifts made up for our financial deficit, and my faith grew. Each change and challenge in life has its difficulties, but as I walked in faith and served God rather than people, my faith strengthened.

God continued to build His church, and He brought a new couple into the fold. They were living together without marriage, but God's word transformed the woman's life. She left the relationship and moved home with her parents. The man, Jack, was a wealthy contractor, and he was shocked when she walked away from his material wealth to obey God. Deeply moved by her example, he continued to attend church without her, and God took hold of his heart. One day, he invited Rick and me to lunch.

"You really should have a home of your own," Jack said.

"We'd love to," Rick said, "but it isn't a financial option." Rick shared how we had sold our home and used the money while the church got on its feet.

"I'll build the house at my cost," Jack replied.

My jaw almost hit the table. "That's so generous. Thank you!"

Rick slid his plate toward the center of the table and leaned forward. "We probably still can't afford it."

"Just go and have a look at the models," Jack said.

In faith, we visited the models, but they were more than we needed. All we wanted was a home designed to accommodate our ministry. We learned of an older model at a different location. It was the least expensive of the models, and it offered the perfect layout. I walked through room after room trying to restrain my excitement. Even with the offer to build at his cost, obtaining a loan and coming up with a down payment seemed insurmountable.

A few weeks later, we sat around the pool at a friend's house enjoying a cookout. A couple who had stopped coming to the church appeared, and we greeted one another and caught up on the latest news. During the course of conversation, they handed us an envelope. "We feel God wants us to give this to you," they said.

My heartbeat quickened. Could this be part of the financial answer? Later, in our van, we opened the envelope. Rick slipped his finger beneath the flap and peeked inside. "I don't believe it."

"What?"

He handed me the envelope with tears in his eyes.

I pulled a check for $5,000 out of the envelope. That money provided the minimum $2,000 down payment and closing costs.

With that gift, our dream house became a reality. We lived there for a little more than ten years. It became known for fellowship and ministry until the time God led us to move to Georgia—without a secured job. Scary business. We believed God and put our house on the market. Our gift house sold during the real estate slump of 2006 with a sizeable profit.

We recouped everything we had given up in Illinois and even more, and when we arrived in Georgia, after much prayer, we found a house and paid for it in full.

The real reward in serving the Lord hasn't been our material gain. It's been a stronger faith and eternal inheritance. Our part has been obedience. We just needed to remember that God has an eye for detail.

—Donna Sunblad

A Nickel
and a Prayer

*And we know that God causes everything to work
together for the good of those who love God and
are called according to his purpose for them.*

Romans 8:28

"Sorry, Madam," the German gate agent said matter-of-factly, peering over his horn-rimmed glasses. My heart sank as he slid our four passports and standby tickets across the counter. "The flight to America is full. Try again tomorrow."

If there's one thing an airline pilot's wife knows well, it's getting bumped off of a flight. So what was with my shock-and-awe reaction? Why the racing pulse, and sinking heart? For one thing, I felt responsible for the precious family and friends I had brought on this European adventure: my daughter, her husband, and a special friend who was grieving a loss and needing a respite. For another, we were virtually out of money; our carefully calculated budget had not considered an extra day.

We gathered in a circle to pray and then collected our belongings and headed to . . . well, we weren't sure. Where *do* folks go when their Plan A, the one that involved wolfing down wiener schnitzel with plastic forks at an altitude of 10,000 feet, leads to their being grounded? We believed God would answer our prayers—but how?

Frankfurt airport offered its usual fare of bustling crowds, kaleidoscope colors, and a smorgasbord of foreign languages. Arriving downstairs, we decided on a time and place to regroup, and we headed off in different directions, lugging bags and secretly wishing for a small wad of cash to drop from the ceiling, like Groucho Marx's duck. We didn't need "quail," just enough "manna" to get us through the next twenty-four hours.

I trudged along a busy corridor, praying for God's wisdom and favor, knowing He could work it all together for good. No sooner had I said, "Amen," than, over the din, I heard the familiar sound of someone speaking Italian. Oh, how the language and people had captivated my heart a decade earlier when we lived among them, and how I missed that memorable sound. It came from an elderly woman behind me. She was visibly distressed, her hands flailing with emotion. A petite, teenage girl with flowing dark hair and a pained expression kept pace beside her.

My heart melted. My mind managed to rustle up and dust off enough schoolbook Italian to offer comfort to the troubled woman, and I ushered her and her oversized tapestry handbag to a nearby chair. I learned she was called Nona, and her Spanish granddaughter accompanying her was Marita. I knelt down and took her hand. "Signora, come puo aiutarla?" *How can I help you?*

Punctuated by sobs, their story flowed from Nona's quivering lips—a tale of lost tickets, a missed flight, and luggage that was nowhere to be found. This precious pair had lost all hope of ever finding their belongings or returning to Rome. I felt ill equipped to help, but compelled to try, and I silently cried out to the Lord for His grace and guidance. I had no clue where to start, but I stood up and took Marita's hand to leave, assuring Nona we would be back.

I know this sounds strange, but it was almost as if I were being led by bridle and bit, up and down escalators, along corridors, past mobs of travelers with this sweet young Spanish girl in tow. It felt as though God held the reins, and I was to follow His lead, as He called me to step out in obedience and faith.

We arrived at a basement claims counter in a remote corner of the terminal. The German agent looked me squarely in the eye and waited for meaningful words to tumble out of my mouth. Unfortunately, my brain was busy trying to recall enough of my four years of high school Spanish to understand Marita, as well as enough of my four semesters of college German for the agent to understand me. My words stumbled over each other, and within minutes, it had become painfully obvious I was out of my league, and we were in trouble. *Help, Lord!*

A well-dressed, middle-aged man approached, having overheard our conversation. In a pleasant manner, he began conversing fluently with each of us in our own languages. He asked questions—mine in English, Marita's in Spanish—and gave our answers to the agent in German, who placed phone calls and kept typing. At last, a machine whirred, spitting out documents and forms.

Our team effort was successful! The bags were all located and would be rerouted to the Rome airport; baggage claim vouchers and two new flight tickets were issued. The agent handed everything to me, and grins erupted across everyone's face. I knew we could have never succeeded without the kind gentleman's help, and I turned to thank him. But he had vanished, as suddenly as he had appeared. I don't pretend to understand God's ways, I only know they are grand and I am grateful.

Marita's grandmother was right where we had left her, looking much like a fragile rag doll slumped in the chair, clutching her handbag. "Nona!" Marita called out, waving the new tickets that would get them home. Our beaming faces told the rest of the story.

I escorted them upstairs to the appropriate ticket counter, explained everything to the English-speaking agent and handed her the documents. She assured me she would take these dear ladies under her wing, so it was time to say goodbye. We hugged. Nona was weeping again, this time with joy. "Grazie a Dios!" she said repeatedly, raising her praying hands and tear-filled eyes upward. *Yes—thank you, God!*

We hugged again and I had turned to leave, when Nona grabbed my arm. She rummaged through her giant handbag to give me something, possibly a coin or two. I tried to resist, but she pressed an object into my hand and closed it firmly. "Prego!" she insisted. *Please!* I thanked her, and we smiled back at each other as I glided down the escalator.

When they were out of sight, I opened my hand to find an American dollar. *Bless her heart*, I thought— *maybe her last.* I choked back tears at the notion and looked again. Two zeroes appeared this time—a $100 bill! I joined my loved ones at our designated spot, and we all praised God, rejoicing over His creative provision. Then we flew into action. We rented a car, drove to the American air base, found two rooms, and bought enough food to last until the next afternoon. In the process of budgeting our new resources, we entered into negotiations with a fellow customer at the store. "Do you need the full dozen eggs? Can we buy half?" Six was all we needed, and all we could afford. He conceded with a smile.

The next day, we stepped onto the plane with one nickel to spare. I taped it onto a card with these words: "A reminder of the power and faithfulness of God— who works all things together for good, to those who love Him and are called according to His purpose."

These days, we travel with credit cards and cell phones to avoid such predicaments. But I'm thankful to have had the privilege of watching the hand of God bring together two sets of people, from different corners of the world, with the same basic need—to find their way home. I'm thankful we saw how miraculously He met everyone's needs in answer to all our prayers. And I'm thankful that you and I can rest assured that when it's all said and done, His promises prevail over our problems. When we are faithful to our God, He is faithful to His word.

—*Sandi L. Banks*

The Musical

Jesus looked at them intently and said,
"Humanly speaking, it is impossible. But
with God everything is possible."

Matthew 19:26

My official title in our tiny church was director of the children's choir, but we all knew my real job was keeping the kids entertained while their parents attended the Wednesday night service. No special talent was necessary for the position: just a love for kids, lots of patience, and the ability to carry a tune. I had a couple of helpers who assisted me in keeping about a dozen children from ages two through twelve in line. Most of the kids were related to each other in some way or another (including my own two children), so I could usually rely on a family member to threaten to "tell Mom." Basically, the job was a no-brainer.

My search for *The Musical* began on a cold, gray afternoon in January. Our Christmas musical was behind us, and I had run out of things for my little choir to do. One day, I took the opportunity to check out the local Christian supply store while my own kids were in school. Winding my way through the aisles of the huge store, I finally found the section on children's ministries. The selection of musicals, plays, and activities was amazing and overwhelming.

For more than two hours, I examined the choices in front of me, waiting to feel that familiar "nudge" from the Lord to give me direction. Nothing. As I stood there, I breathed a silent prayer for help and tried to listen. Still nothing. So, I read plays, reviewed material for activities, and listened to music. Nothing jumped out as being extraordinary. In desperation, I finally chose a play I thought we could do. Nothing very exciting, but I was tired of looking, and the kids would be getting home from school soon. It was then I heard it. "Write it. Write a musical." No voice, no thunder, no burning bush. Just a soft, insistent knowing in my heart. "Write it."

After an hour of trying to put the thought out of my mind, I put my chosen play back on the shelf and drove home empty-handed. As soon as I got through the front door of my house, I called the director of children's ministries. "Becky? You know how I'm trying to find a project for the kids to do on Wednesday night? Well, this is going to sound crazy but I think the Lord wants me to write a musical."

"Great!" she replied.

"But, Becky, you know I can't write music. I can barely even read it. I have no training or experience."

She laughed. "Sounds like a God thing to me. Go for it!"

After dinner, homework, TV time, and putting the kids to bed, I sat in my big brown chair. I was exhausted, but still hoping for some kind of direction or inspiration: an idea, a song, a hint, or a word. Anything. I sat in silence and waited for an idea. Nothing. And then, the quiet, persistent voice in my mind I had heard earlier that day returned, and I knew I needed to put the pen to paper. I put the point of the pen to the notebook in my lap. I must be losing it, I thought.

The moment my pen touched the paper, a world of ideas flew into my head. Characters, scenery, plot, lighting, and music filled my vision. Never had I composed with such clarity. Never had I known so firmly or been so sure of what I was doing. The pen flew across the page as I drew staff after staff of melody lines. By the end of only three hours, I had outlined the plot, sketched the costumes and scenery, defined the characters, and written three songs. The official title would be *Christian Army*, but the work would forever be referred to simply as *The Musical*.

During the next three weeks, I would get the kids off to school and write *The Musical*. Dialogue flowed as characters emerged and became friends: Corporal Faith, Major Miracle, and Colonel Wisdom. When it was finished, the Lord had provided our little children's choir with an hour-long musical, complete with nine songs, dialogue, and parts that fit each one of the children in the choir.

After putting the final touches on *The Musical* and getting clearance from our pastor and elders, I gathered the choir together and began rehearsals. Children who I had never known could sing took on solo parts, and kids who had barely spoken in class belted out dialogue as if they were on a Broadway stage.

It took another four months to produce the final version of *The Musical*, which the children performed to a packed house on Father's Day. Our little troop had grown from twelve to almost thirty, as people in the area discovered that our church had a children's choir on Wednesday nights. The kids sang their hearts out, the youth group worked the sound system, lighting, and sets, and my daughter's piano teacher provided accompaniment. The audience laughed, cried, and applauded, as if they were hearing something truly special, and we all knew it was.

We only performed *The Musical* once. For some reason, we all knew it was finished when the last song was sung on Father's Day. We went on to do other projects as a choir and continued to stay busy on Wednesday nights. Although *The Musical* was copyrighted, it was never published. One song made it to the stage of a large church in town after their music director heard it and asked to use it for worship services. Every once in awhile, I find myself absent-mindedly humming a tune, and I always smile when I realize it's one of the songs from *The Musical*.

I have no idea what part *The Musical* played in the Lord's great plan. I don't really know if anyone came to know Jesus because of it, or if any of the children went on to become musicians. I do know that something happened in my heart and in the hearts of the kids in our choir. We learned firsthand not to despise small beginnings. And we learned that, regardless of what you think your limitations are, "with God everything is possible." Even for a little Wednesday night choir.

—*Victoria Hart*

Digging in
My Heels

*Ask me and I will tell you remarkable secrets
you do not know about things to come.*

Jeremiah 33:3

As my husband and I were walking out the door to attend a wedding, the phone rang. When I picked up the receiver, I heard our youngest daughter, Christy, begging us to pick up our nine-month-old granddaughter. Our son-in-law had just told Christy he wanted out of their six-year marriage. My adrenalin surged into overdrive while we changed clothes and rushed to their home. Christy ran out the front door with Libby in her arms. "I can't talk now," she said between sobs. "Just please take her back home with you."

The scene devastated me and I silently prayed. *God, I can't leave here without any information. I need to fix this right now!* There was no mistaking the answers that came from my heart. I wouldn't be fixing anything that day. It was simply too much for me to handle alone.

With one phone call, my "white picket fence world" crumbled. I immediately cried out to God, expecting an instant miracle. I had experienced the horrible reality of divorce when my parents split up, and my stomach churned as I relived the hurt, abandonment, and resentment I had felt thirty-five years before.

After several futile days of pleading and reasoning with my daughter and son-in-law, it became apparent that their marriage was beyond repair. Pride and selfishness on both sides ran deep, and I could neither control nor resolve the situation. I asked my friends and family for serious prayer, and I became determined to dig in my heels and grab on to God as I had never done before. I would not relent until the marriage was restored.

I prayed every time I was in my car. I prayed during sleepless nights. I prayed constantly during the day while going through the motions of living. Perhaps my persistence would convince God that He needed to intervene immediately and work a quick resolution. However, things continued to go downhill when my daughter and granddaughter moved in with us.

At that point, God began a work in me that I cherish as a most precious demonstration of grace. He dragged me through his school of complete surrender, and my pitiful attempts to control my life and the lives of my family experienced a sudden death. As I lay flat on my face, I gave up and let God take over. He clutched me in His grip of submission so that I would learn the pure freedom of trust. I had no desire to trust, but out of determined will, I made a decision to do exactly that.

The initial shock waves of crushed dreams led to grim acceptance. Divorce lawyers were hired. Hearing my daughter cry herself to sleep at night wrenched my heart. The empty look in my son-in-law's eyes made me want to hug him and wring his neck at the same time. When my chubby, little granddaughter cooed, "Dada, Dada," I offered up her babbles to God as a prayer for her Daddy. The break up impacted our entire extended family: grandparents, aunts, uncles, cousins, and even close friends. Birthdays and holidays were now hollow celebrations.

In my spiritual naivety, I had assumed God would simply answer my petitions and restore our family. Night after night, I lay in bed longing for relief to come, but nothing of significance occurred. God knew this was not a "quick fix." Changed lives lead to changed circumstances. I wanted changed circumstances; God wanted changed lives.

The truths I learned during this time have stayed with me as treasured gifts. I learned that God is still in control even when my world is crumbling around me. That He can be trusted even when I can't see Him working. I learned I must completely release my children. When I do, God can work with them in His way and in His time without my interference. I must let my adult children develop their own relationship with God, independent of mine.

I learned the power of persistent prayer as I relentlessly begged God to heal my daughter's marriage. Sacrificial, intercessory prayer became a significant part of my life. It took commitment, and it wore me out. Some family and friends advised me to face reality and lay down the fight, but God gave me a passion to keep praying, and that is exactly what I did. He faithfully met me every time I went before Him.

I learned humility. My, did I ever learn humility! The credit I had taken for raising "perfect" children exploded in my prideful face. Now, I am able to see the needs of others with compassion and empathy.

Nearly a year after my daughter's devastating announcement, I received another phone call, this time from my son-in-law. The humble tone of his voice excited me. He began to tell me about a spiritual encounter he had a few days before. He could not explain it, except to say that he felt an overwhelming sense of being lifted up in prayer. I am convinced that all of the prayers for this young man over his entire lifetime, and particularly the petitions of the past year, flowed over him that night like a deluge of healing rain. He said he was ready to take on the responsibility of being a godly husband and father.

Three weeks later, on a warm July night, I looked out my kitchen window and saw my granddaughter asleep in her swing. My daughter and son-in-law sat under a tree nearby—talking, laughing, and forgiving. A miracle had occurred when they both realized the wonder of God's amazing grace in their lives. They renewed their wedding vows in the privacy of their new home several months later, and their marvelous redemption continues today as they are growing in their love for God and for one another.

Do I now trust God with His plan for my family's lives? Not entirely! But after my year of prayer and patience, I have a new tenderness toward Him. I even praise Him for the anguish because, without it, I would not know the intimacy of learning to trust Him. I have been stretched outside the boundaries of what I thought I could endure, and I wouldn't have had it any other way.

—Linda Blaine Powell

When the
Seed Sprouts

So let's not get tired of doing what is good.
At just the right time we will reap a har-
vest of blessing if we don't give up.

Galatians 6:9

I've never been much of a gardener, so I rely mostly
on good fortune and the proper combination of
rain and sunshine to help my garden grow. I would
throw seeds in the soil, along with a bit of fertil-
izer, and I was always amazed when something green
appears. When I realized I had planted my gladiolas upside down, I decided not to dig them all up.
Instead, I simply prayed for them to overcome my
shortcomings as a gardener.

My prayers must have worked because my garden
was graced with the most beautiful gladiolas on the
block. I watched as my neighbors toiled, watered, and

weeded, but truthfully, my garden looked as good as theirs did with much less effort. In fact, I harvested an abundance of roses this year to share with friends. An amazing event, in view of the fact that the only "Miracle Grow" I added was a little prayer.

I believe it's the same with children's ministry. You can plant a seed of faith, combine it with a little prayer, and watch the spiritual growth that takes place. About six years ago, in our congregation of more than 800 people, it appeared that we were short of volunteers. Every Sunday bulletin announced the need for a leader and a teacher for the second-service special needs children.

I had no experience as a Sunday school teacher, let alone any experience with special needs children. I had once met a child with a mild case of cerebral palsy, and here I was giving serious consideration to the position of leading special needs children on Sunday mornings. I wasn't qualified for the job, and I was already working fifty hours every week just to make ends meet.

I prayed about it for two weeks before I finally decided to speak to the children's ministry coordinator. I stepped into her office and announced, "I'm not qualified."

"God will guide you," she said. "You're here, and that's the first step."

"I don't think I can do this."

But she was persistent. "You can. With God's help, all things are possible. These kids need someone with a heart for the Lord more than someone with a degree in education."

Three weeks later, with a little training under my belt, I stepped into the Sunday school classroom to meet my kids. Two of the older girls with autism giggled at me as I fumbled with the doorstop. One of the younger boys, also autistic, sat glued to the television where a VCR tape was playing "Noah's Ark" and had no interest in me at all. A young boy sat at the table alone with his hands folded in front of him. This was Connor and he had been born with Down syndrome. He smiled at me, and I shook his hand as I introduced myself as his new Sunday school teacher. He immediately wanted to help me and started to show me around our classroom. We connected instantly, and I knew I had made the right decision.

Every week for roughly three years, I entered that classroom and sat with the children for about an hour and a half. Some Sundays were harder than others, especially if I had gone through an extremely difficult week at work but, somehow, being with the kids refreshed me. I sang with them in the children's chapel, read them Bible stories, and talked with them about God and the importance of thanking Him for everything. I often wondered how much of the worship was sinking in for Connor.

For one of our Sunday projects we painted a little heart-shaped box. Inside each box, I placed a tiny note that read, "God is Love." I returned the boxes to the children the following Sunday and explained to them that the best way that we can show the world that we are all God's children is to love one another.

When the parents arrived to pick up the children, Connor's mother asked him, "What do you have there?"

He smiled and said, "Miss Shelly gave me this. She loves me." Again, I was left to wonder if he had really grasped the lesson I just taught. I suppose it didn't matter, and in the end, it was enough for him to know that I did love him very much. I had convinced myself that there would be no real breakthrough moments with Connor. There would be no illuminating events that could make God seem real to him, or to any of the special kids.

I think every teacher must sometimes wonder whether or not her teaching is being absorbed. Only time and circumstance would prove if my work with the children was making a difference in their lives. Maybe one day, they would share a story, reach out to the lonely and unwanted, or touch a person's heart in some way. I needed to believe I could make God very personal for them. I wanted them to know they could have an intimate and loving relationship with a very real and loving God. As I reinforced the need to thank God for all of our blessings daily, I prayed that the ritual would develop into the relationship that would change their lives.

The leaves had just begun to turn their autumn shades, and my Sundays with Connor were coming to an end. With the downturn of the economy, Connor's father had lost his job, and the family was being forced to move to Michigan. It was a tearful goodbye, but I knew the family had made the right decision, and we promised to keep in touch. Several years passed with occasional e-mails and postcards from the family and it seemed everyone, even Connor, was adjusting well to their surroundings. His mother e-mailed me last summer to say that Connor had met a "girlfriend" at camp, and the two of them could be seen holding hands everywhere they went. The family had found a new church home and attended regularly.

A few months ago, I heard from Connor's mother again. She had returned home from the store and heard praise music playing in his room. She peeked in and saw him on his knees, hands raised above his head, singing and praising the Lord. She closed the door quietly and went downstairs to write me a letter.

"Dear Shelly, You will never know, could never know, what a difference you made in my child's life. I know there must have been days when you felt it wasn't sinking in, but you were planting seeds and what a harvest we are reaping today! Connor is helping hand out church bulletins on Sunday mornings, and he is a greeter at church. His smile lights up the sanctuary. When he sings, the whole congregation cannot drown him out. You will never know how you touched his life. He spends every afternoon after school in his room, listening to worship and praise music and giving thanks to God. Just as you taught him to do—to give thanks every day. May you continue to be richly blessed, Love, Kathy."

Tears streamed down my cheeks. I never knew he was soaking up so much of God's word. Just like my garden, I had planted the seed in Connor and left the rest up to God. There were Sundays when I didn't think it was worth the effort and days when my body ached and my head hurt. I showed up in the classroom anyway, and trusted the Lord. I didn't give up, and I was blessed with the privilege of watching Connor grow into a lovely garden for God.

—*Michele Starkey*

The Peace Cottage

Don't worry about anything; instead, pray about everything. Tell God what you need, and thank him for all he has done. Then you will experience God's peace, which exceeds anything we can understand. His peace will guard your hearts and minds as you live in Christ Jesus.

Philippians 4:6–7

A somber mood prevailed that Saturday as a few friends helped me load my life into a U-Haul. Furniture and the stuff of daily life filled the waiting truck. Many of the boxes contained possessions tucked away for another time and another place. I had packed away dreams of what might have been, though most of my dreams lay in a crumpled heap at the bottom of my heart. My marriage of twenty-eight years was over.

My husband and I had planned to build a spacious home, the kind you anticipate when the nest empties and retirement becomes a reality. Now those house plans, rolled and dusty, occupied a corner of the garage, and I was moving into a house a quarter its size.

Feeling too old to start over and too afraid to put much effort into it, I latched onto a rental house available through my daughter's landlord. The neighborhood would never have been my choice. Further, the floors of the funky cottage sloped southward, and the kitchen sported walls and a ceiling the color of orange sherbet. If I stood on tiptoes, I could brush the ceilings with my fingertips, but I moved in.

To my surprise and delight, certain items of furniture fit perfectly, and soon, the little place started to possess a charm of its own. Lace curtains graced the windows, antique and family pictures dotted the walls, and a new quilt draped my downsized bed. Two tall bookcases bulged with volumes, and even the kitchen met my approval when I added perky window valances. And who would notice the ceiling anyway?

But cozy soon threatened to turn into cramped, so numerous boxes, the additional furniture, and the miscellaneous accumulation of decades filled a storage unit. Although that proved a good temporary solution, the monthly cost would not be wise in the long term. Why did I own all this stuff, anyway, and what should I do with it? Possibilities swirled through my weary mind: the dump, local charities, and an instant garage sale with everything priced "best offer."

Even though I knew God didn't want me to worry, anxiety became my unwelcome roommate. I tried to remember that His desire for me lay in praying and trusting Him for my life and its outcome but, in those early days, I often paced the floor with my arms wrapped around myself in a protective gesture.

After a couple of months of settling in, I began to relax and came up with the idea to name my little place. My life lay in turmoil and I sought peace—God's peace. I envisioned quiet evenings on the couch with my Bible, a good book or movie, or a quilting project. Soon, my friends came to know my new residence as The Peace Cottage.

Like any project worth taking on, living in God's peace didn't happen in an instant. Bit by bit, I released my fears, although too often I reclaimed them and wrestled once more. I had to acknowledge that dreams die, but God is not one who allows voids or vacancies. With the death of old dreams, new visions shine forth. And that's what happened over time.

One of my biggest breakthroughs came when I complained to the Lord about my lack of space and money. Abruptly, I remembered to be thankful, but I realized I had to quit grousing to express my gratitude. My new location proved more than safe, and my neighbors became friends. We shared casual chats and extra food. Funds were tight, but my savings still provided a cushion and my bills were paid. My health couldn't be better. Family and friends surrounded me with incomprehensible love, and my new church welcomed me and nurtured me through my pain.

However, the storage unit remained full, and I'd written out more monthly rental checks than I cared to admit. I knew I needed to let go of some things, but I also knew that process would take time. My values resided at a deeper level than just my possessions, yet being surrounded by family treasures, quilts, and books brought a measure of security and helped me find balance in my shattered world. Their beauty and familiarity helped me gain a sense of place in this uncharted territory called single life. So I continued to pay for the storage unit and focused first on the muddled state of my mind and emotions.

After a while, I sensed God's nudging, reminding me it was finally time to pare down my possessions and generate some income. I rolled up my sleeves and dug through boxes. Two garage sales, many donation loads, plus a few full garbage cans equaled notable progress. Diligence at the computer with my writing, as well as a home sales business, helped fill in the monetary gaps.

God loves to surprise and delight His children, and He threw in a few bonuses—a secret gift to offset the cost of a writer's conference, friends who contributed gas money, and a donated airline ticket to visit my sister in New York. Such gifts served to strengthen my faith and assure me that I was loved.

Most of the time my life lives up to the essence of my home's name. God's promise is for peace, but some days I totter on the brink of discouragement and despondency. I still struggle with His command to "pray about everything." Telling Him what I need is the easy part, but thanking Him when I feel more grouchy than grateful requires a spiritual stretch. Yet, when I make the effort to be thankful first, then spill out my concerns, His comfort settles my heart. I hum through the days, confident He's on patrol in my heart and mind.

My life has been irreparably changed, and my future remains uncertain, but trust in God has allowed peace to replace anxiety as my live-in companion. My Peace Cottage is open to my new neighbor-friends, as well as old friends and family. I hosted my daughter's wedding rehearsal dinner and have sipped tea or shared meals with friends at my table. My granddaughter chants, "Nana. Out," the moment her parents turn the corner onto my street. She knows my home as a place of love and security and wants out of her baby seat so the two of us can hug and play.

As planned, I've curled up on the couch to enjoy a good read, watch a few movies, and finish several quilts. My world, once shrunken to fit in the back of a rental truck, has expanded and brought with it hope and new dreams for a secure future. At the moment, I have no plans to move. No matter the duration, I'll remember my time in The Peace Cottage as a season of transition from devastation and hopelessness to serenity and the assurance of continued safety if I allow myself to trust God for His protection.

—*Lynn Ludwick*

So, You Think
You Had a Bad Day?

*Dear brothers and sisters, when troubles come
your way, consider it an opportunity for great joy.
For you know that when your faith is tested, your
endurance has a chance to grow. So let it grow,
for when your endurance is fully developed, you
will be perfect and complete, needing nothing.*

James 1:2–4

When I arrived to visit Mother in the hospital, her preacher was about to finish a forlorn recitation of his trials that day. I entered the room just in time to catch his last few words, "and then the second car's battery died."

Mother and I exchanged glances, and I restrained myself from adding my two cents. "Life's little, or large, inconveniences aren't the same as true troubles."

We had lived longer than he had, our faith had been tested more times, and our endurance had experienced more opportunities to grow. Although we might have been a bit closer to achieving the illusive "letting our troubles become opportunities for joy," we knew we still had much to learn about fulfilling the principle of James 1:2–4 in our lives.

After he left, Mother and I joked about our human tendency to share a litany of misfortunes at inopportune times and to somehow believe our own experiences are more difficult than those of our neighbor. "Are we in competition to win the title of 'The Best of the Worst of Days?'" I asked, and Mother laughed.

At times, we mirror the unspoken belief that if we are God's children, then He will shield us from life's difficulties. Scripture clearly states the opposite. "Here on Earth you will have many trials and sorrows. But take heart, because I have overcome the world" (John 16:33b). John tells us that we will have troubles; James teaches us how to grow through them.

Mother and I had both lost sons to the AIDS epidemic, so in the hospital that day we discussed how losing a child had given us a different perspective on life's "inconveniences." Still, we understood how inconveniences could be truly frightening and how difficult it could be to turn a bad day into an opportunity to discover joy.

"Speaking of inconveniences," Mother said, "do you remember your *own* experiences that day you left our house to return to Phoenix?"

I grimaced. "Do I remember? How could I ever forget it?" A quick slide show of memories flashed through my mind.

Our family of six had flown to my parents' home in Tennessee. The day before we were scheduled to return home, our eleven-year-old diabetic son had to be hospitalized. Our bargain tickets allowed no changes, so we left John in his grandparents' care and returned home without him.

Cheap tickets also meant a late-night flight. After boarding, my husband went to the bathroom, and I quickly dozed off. When I awoke, I realized he still hadn't returned to his seat. I glanced up front where there appeared to a lot of unusual activity. When I looked closer, I recognized Jim's body sprawled across the front row. Leaping over several seats of sleeping children in a single bound, I claimed the white-as-a-sheet man as my husband.

One of the hostesses explained. "He passed out, and we've phoned for an ambulance to meet the plane."

When we landed, I gave my now conscious and embarrassed husband a quick kiss before the ambulance departed. Two down and four to go, I thought, as I gathered my three sleepy kids and their carry-on luggage before herding everyone off to baggage claim.

After retrieving six suitcases, we trudged toward the car. Pulling heavy luggage and dragging cranky children, I finally arrived at the spot where we had left the car the week before.

It wasn't there. At first, I panicked, and then I wondered if I had forgotten where we left it. I looked around until I found a helpful attendant. "I'm so sorry, ma'am, but we resurfaced that lot and towed all the vehicles left in it. Come with me, and we'll find your car."

Our car was found, and at 3:00 A.M., accompanied by my parade of bleary-eyed kids and luggage, I breathed a sigh of relief. During twenty-two hours of travel we had "lost" two family members, found one car, and were now close to home. I smiled at my little troopers. "It won't be long now kids. You'll be in your own beds in twenty minutes." I have since learned the foolishness of making such promises—especially to children.

"Mom, what's that hissing sound?" said the winner of the I-get-the-front-seat-competition. Three pairs of tired eyes stared at me, and I stared at the temperature gauge.

"Hot!" it announced with a bright orange glow.

The tow truck, which had moved our car to the second lot, had punctured a hole in the radiator. All the water had drained out, and even though I had a trunk-full of stuff, I did not have the gallons of water we usually kept there for emergency use in Phoenix's extreme heat.

"Wait here," I commanded before I cautiously left the car to use a pay phone at a nearby service station. I was more than tired and sleepy, more than worried and angry: I was scared to death.

I confess I did not look for joy in those pressing conditions. Furthermore, I had experienced more growth in character-building than I could stomach in one twenty-four hour period. I did whisper a prayer, "God, please keep us safe," and He did. I had chosen the quickest, most direct route home, but one that led straight through Phoenix's red light district. God was surely with us, because I never saw a solitary soul on the streets.

An eternity passed in the pay phone booth. When our sleepy preacher finally answered his phone, I sobbed and, rapidly, nearly incoherently, poured out the events of the night. I had no shame when I begged, "Please, will you come take us home?"

We waited another twenty long minutes, praying and keeping a wary eye on our surroundings. He arrived, transferred our bodies and bags into his car, and headed out to the suburbs. I don't recall being concerned about leaving the car to the thieves who also roamed that part of town until I came to my senses the next afternoon and finally called for a tow truck.

My body sagged with relief as our house came into view. The euphoric feeling lasted until I opened the front door to find our entrance hall ceiling resting on top of a soaking-wet carpet. That was just before I discovered the majority of the gravel from our flat roof in the swimming pool. It now resembled a dirty, rocky creek bed.

"We had torrential rains and a wind storm while you were gone," our preacher said. He left us with another offer of help. "If there's anything else I can do, please let me know."

I called the hospital to check on Jim. After the nurse assured me he was resting comfortably, I did what any self-respecting Southern woman would do. I tucked my children in and went straight to bed myself, subscribing to the wisdom of Scarlett O'Hara. "I'll think about it all tomorrow."

However, it was several years before I thought of days like this one as being among those that strengthened my character and caused me to grow in faith and trust in God. I had endured, and I was more than fine. The time came when I could even laugh at the memory.

Still, God was not finished shaping my character. In 2001, after years of enjoying great health, abundant energy, and a wonderful job, I was deluged with a series of health problems that left me in debilitating chronic pain, with a minimum of energy even on the best of days, and relying on a disability check for needed income.

As I have reflected on God's promises during this latest time of struggle, I know I have grown as a Christian, thanks to His leading me through paths I would never have chosen to walk myself. I have great joy in my Lord. He has been faithful to me in the past, so I know He will be faithful to His promises in the future. I have no doubt that He will continue to guide and direct me, shaping me into a fuller image of Him day by day, if I recall His promises and follow His lead.

Today, as I continue living, reading, and studying His word, I realize that the kind of testing which produced endurance and character in the lives of first-century Christians is a type about which I know nothing at all. They would probably view my worst troubles as minor inconveniences, and I'm quite sure those blessed souls could easily say, "So you think *you've* had some bad days?!"

—*Elaine Young McGuire*

Freely Receive,
Freely Give

*God blesses those who are merci-
ful, for they will be shown mercy.*

Matthew 5:7

One winter, a long time ago, I came to understand in more completeness and depth how much giving to others glorifies God and in turn blesses the giver.

"Do you want to come into town with me?" My dad grunted as he struggled to put on his winter coat. His broad shoulders barely fit the jacket; I thought the coat might rip in two. He fastened the buttons and reached for his funny red hat with the flaps that covered the ears and the bonnet-like tie below the chin. He turned toward me, the sides of his hat flapping like wings. "You coming?" He reminded me of Elmer Fudd, ready for a hunt.

White clouds of frozen fluff blew by the picture window. The song "It's Beginning to Look a Lot Like Christmas" played in my head. Despite the frigid temperature, the outdoors looked inviting. Then again, at the age of eight, anything that released me from the cooped-up house and my three siblings sounded inviting. "Sure!" The excitement in my voice couldn't be hidden. I grabbed my coat and hat and ran to take my seat as co-captain in dad's pickup.

We pulled out of the driveway, new snow crunching under the weight of the truck. My dad paid the weather no mind. He engaged the four-wheel drive and, together, we plowed through the storm.

"Where are we going?" I asked, as the bumpy road tossed me into the air. I had purposely loosened my seatbelt so my head would brush the hood of the cab with each major dip.

"We're going to do something nice for someone who's less fortunate."

What? I didn't get the clothes I wanted for school this year. Who can be less fortunate than that? I sat still, closed my mouth, and continued to bounce up and down.

"Your father has a special gift," my mother used to say. My dad did have a wonderful ability to put others first. He used to show my siblings and me, with deeds more than words, the importance of giving. With little effort, he could be truly selfless.

One of my favorite stories about my dad's merciful spirit came from his childhood. He grew up on a farm in south central Nebraska, the tenth of thirteen children. Money couldn't have been scarcer for his large farm family. By the time my father was a young man, my grandpa's health had significantly declined. As a result, my dad, a 6'4" all-muscle farm boy, gave up any opportunity to play sports in high school. "My father needed me on the farm," he told me. "Even when the basketball coach hunted me down during my sophomore year and gave me a hard time, the football coach stood up for me. He said, 'Let him be; he's got his priorities straight.' I would have liked to have gone out for sports, but I knew I had to help your grandpa."

Dad drove over the snow-packed streets of our small town. He carefully parked the truck in front of one of the only two banks. After securing the brake, he hopped out and onto the slick sidewalk. The engine continued to run with the heater on full blast. A few minutes later, he returned. With head down, he held on tight to his flapping hat while gripping his coat. The wintry wind blew into the cab as he yanked open the driver's door.

"So, what *are* we doing?" My lips were so cold, I could barely part them to ask the question.

"You'll see." He smiled. "You look chilly. Put your hands near the heater." He chuckled at my suscepti-bility to the cold. Easy for him to say. Blood as thick as peanut butter ran through his veins. At times, he went out in the dead of winter with only a light jacket, and he would still break a sweat. I heeded his advice and leaned forward with my lips practically touching the vent. Warm air never felt so wonderful. Dad shifted the truck into gear and we continued on our journey.

Just outside town lay a farmhouse. Peeling paint hung from the siding. A broken fence and screen door needed fixing, and stuff lay scattered around the yard. I didn't recognize the place at the time. Dad told me that the young couple living there had small children and were trying to support themselves as best they could by raising hogs. The market showed no leniency in those days to small operation pig farmers. Although the couple had never asked for handouts, my dad was the local livestock feed salesman, and he was aware of their financial predicament.

He parked in front of the small dwelling. Hope and mercy seemed to overflow from deep within his spirit. The air held such thick anticipation I found myself antsy with excitement. I watched as my dad opened his jacket and pulled out the envelope from the bank. He took out a stack of bills—more money than I had ever seen. He took a plastic, padded manila envelope from under the armrest and stuffed the bills inside. Then he sealed the opening with one quick lick and reached for the door handle. "Stay in here," he said. "I'll be right back."

Once again, I sat still and said nothing. My eyes followed dad as he battled the cold wind and blustery snow. He looked like a dark pen mark on a white piece of paper. As he walked, he once again held his hat and coat close. Soon, the white wall erased him. In no time, he reappeared and jumped back into the cab. He shivered, and I watched him rub his big hands against his arms to try to warm himself.

"What did you do, Dad?"

After his dry, chapped hands were thoroughly warmed, he dusted the powdery snow off his coat. The stubborn flakes stayed on the seat next to me, defying the threat of heat. Then he took a deep breath and turned my way. Small pools of tears had gathered at the corners of his eyes. "See that house?" He pointed out the front window. "Those people have endured hardships of late, and I wanted to help."

"But they don't know you left them anything. Are they even home?" *And we don't have much more than they do.*

He smiled. "No. I made sure they weren't home. It's no fun to give if the person feels obligated to give back." With that, he drove away from the barren farm. In slow silence, we trudged through the deepening snow toward home.

I had played a small part as a witness to God's promise revealed, that one winter day.

As the years passed, there were many occasions when my family had a need and God provided. Often, His provision was bountiful. I believe this occurred in part to God's promise to show mercy to those who are merciful at heart—just like my dad.

—*L. A. Lindburgh*

Digging for Treasure

My child, pay attention to what I say,
Listen carefully to my words.
Don't lose sight of them.
Let them penetrate deep into your heart
For they bring life to those who find them,
And healing to their whole body.

Proverbs 4:20–22

"Bibles up," the Sunday school teacher announced.

I gripped my Bible's cover and thrust my hand into the air.

"Proverbs 4:20–22. Ready?"

With my feet anchored to the ground and leveraged by the chair's legs, I focused my eyes on the teacher's mouth—waiting for just one word. "Go!"

Thud! My Bible hit my lap and like a puppy frantically searching for its morning meal, my mad dash to find the verse began. I knew exactly where to find Proverbs. *This was an easy one.* Adrenaline pumped through me as my fingers found Proverbs and flipped through the pages.

With a jerk, I bolted out of my seat and rattled off words like an auctioneer, "My child, pay attention to what I say. Listen carefully to my words. Don't lose sight of them. Let them penetrate deep into your heart for they bring life to those who find them, and healing to their whole body." Victory! I plopped in my seat. *Once again, I won!*

I loved Bible sword drills in Sunday school and could find verses faster than anyone else. Some of the verses the teacher called out were ones I had memorized, but reciting them wasn't as important as finding them first. If someone else won a round, I insisted we do it again. I had to win again.

My child, pay attention to what I say.

Listen carefully to my words.

Years later, more Bibles adorned my shelf, but difficulty, trials, and sorrow filled my heart. The Bibles stood for the words and chapters I had memorized in my youth, while my struggles represented a constant onslaught of pain that sword drill winnings couldn't relieve. *What can soothe this ruthless ache in my heart?*

I gobbled up the pages of Christian self-help books, looking for solutions to the difficulties I faced. I eagerly put methods and formulas into practice, but my problems lingered, so I bought another book, and another, and another. One after another, I devoured the authors' words looking for a remedy. None provided any long-term benefit. Frustration settled in for an extended visit, and God became a silent and distant being.

God, where are you? Do you even care? As soon as the questions left my mouth, I returned to the formula-filled books, and a pattern began to emerge. Every time scripture appeared, I skipped over the verses, anxious to discover what the author had to say next. *I've known that verse since I was kid.* But like a splinter trying to wiggle its way out, the pattern began to irritate me and demand my attention. *Why do I value the author's words over God's truths? Why don't the words I memorized long ago have anything to do with my life today?* I didn't have an answer, but I suspected God knew more than any human author.

God, where do I begin? How do I find You? Sure, I may have known the exact spot in my Bible to find Malachi, but there had to be more to the Bible than the goal of locating a verse. Just finding it didn't solve my problems. Formulas didn't last. Humbled, I put my self-help books on hold and picked up my Bible instead. Not with the intent to be first, but desperate to find solace and support in the words I knew so well. I longed to apply God's words to my life.

Don't lose sight of them.
Let them penetrate deep into your heart.

I delved into the Bible, read the annotations provided, and jotted down notes on the verses that caught my attention. But within a few days, I forgot their importance and application. *God, how do I stay close to You?* I tried to be still in my prayer time, but my mind wandered to my endless "to do" list and the problems weighing on my heart. *Help me! I wander so easily.*

My budding relationship with God required perseverance, not a Sunday ride with cruise control. It required action on my part. God wasn't silent. He was merely waiting for me to desire more of a relationship with Him. *What is my motivation? To seek an answer or learn more about God?* I set aside anything that interfered—even my problems.

I wrote certain verses on paper, and pasted them in places I repeatedly visited: the bathroom mirror, my desk, by my bed, and even on the dashboard of my car. I wrote out my prayers to help me stay focused. I took time to just be still. I imagined myself sitting at God's feet with no burdens to carry. I sought Him throughout my entire day, not just during one designated time. No longer was God a casual visitor in my heart's home. He was settling into permanent residency.

For they bring life to those who find them,
And healing to their whole body.

Soon, my ten-minute quiet time felt too short. It grew to fifteen minutes, then twenty and even more as time became irrelevant. I found myself reciting the truths and promises of the Bible naturally in situations, not out of habit of memorization, but as a result of taking time to seek and apply their genuine meaning for my life. Finally, I became able to take true aim at my precious goal—to open the door of my heart and let God and His words find their resting place within me.

Now, I still grab my Bible daily. It isn't a race, and I don't need a formula. Instead, I am motivated to nourish my fellowship with God by reading His word. Without Him, I am nothing. Without Him, I lack purpose and meaning. Without Him, burdens overwhelm my life.

When my relationship with God began to flourish, my problems didn't vanish; at times, new ones surfaced. Many of my unanswered questions remained unanswered. However, the importance of finding God overshadowed my need to win, or find a solution to my problems. In my quest to find God, I received peace in the storms of life, rest during the weary journey, comfort when life didn't make sense, and internal healing—even in the darkest places hidden in my heart.

—*Karla Kassebaum*

Four Calves
A-Leaping

*But for you who fear my name, the Sun
of Righteousness will rise with healing
in his wings. And you will go free, leaping with joy like calves let out to pasture.*

Malachi 4:2

Spiritual highs are not uncommon to the Christian experience. They have often been compared
to Moses' encounter with the Almighty on Mount
Sinai, or the disciples' journey to the mountain of
transfiguration with Jesus. But as most of us know,
what goes up usually comes down. I'm referring to
the inevitable valley at the bottom of the mountain. Moses discovered it when he descended Mount
Sinai only to be met by an unruly band of Israelites.
The disciples found their "valley" when they came
down the mountain to run headlong into immediate

persecution. However, scripture and experience have proven that God uses these spiritual highs and lows for our ultimate good.

After one of these highs, my valley came rather abruptly. I was on my way home from my first writers' conference in the mountains of New Mexico. Imagine the high of fellowshipping with 300 like-minded Christians, all with a common passion for expressing God's truths through the written word. On the four-hour drive home, my thoughts were swirling with exciting information, and I began to immediately rethink the plot of a novel I'd been working on. My new story grew more ingenious with every mile. I couldn't wait to get home and get to work. In one of the small towns between the conference and home, I braked for a red light, and that's when all my plans plunged to Earth.

While I waited, I fiddled with the radio dial for a moment before I glanced up to check the light. Right in front of me, impossible to miss, was my estranged sister. She was on a bicycle, her eyes staring straight ahead. I hadn't spoken to her in over two years, but during that nanosecond of time, I knew God had something to tell me. For years, I had rehearsed my litany of grievances against my sister, and my heart had become hardened. Now, the issue had become a stumbling block to my fellowship with God, and I knew it had to be resolved before He could entrust me with the call to write.

Forgiving her had been a long struggle, and persistent prayer brought me no lasting peace. I assured God and myself many times that I had truly forgiven her, but before I knew it, old memories and grudges returned to taunt me. A few days after returning from the conference, I prayed again with even more determination. It occurred to me that I should make a list of my complaints against my sibling and ask God to help me toss them as far as the east is from the west, to remember them no more.

With a renewed sense of awe, I realized something very important. God may not have literally forgotten my sins, but I knew He no longer held those transgressions against me. His promise, "Therefore there is now no condemnation," became even more real. Using this simple principle, I wrote a list of grievances and tossed it toward the east—coincidentally, where my wastebasket was located. Then came the hard part. To complete my commitment, I needed to communicate forgiveness to my sister. I didn't know how I would accomplish my task or what I would say. So I did what I do best—I tried to put it off.

A week later, I received a call from a friend. "You never told me you had a sister," she said.

Her words took my breath away. Obviously, God was not going to let me procrastinate. My friend said she had met my dad at the nursing home where he lived, and he expressed a desire to be reconciled with his estranged daughter. I was too embarrassed to tell my friend I wasn't speaking to my sister, and before I could stop myself, I promised her I would relay my father's message. Boy, did I ever walk into that one! I knew my friend planned to visit my father again, and she would hold me to the promise.

The next morning, I sat down reluctantly and wrote my sister a short note expressing our father's wishes. Before I signed it, I included my own desire to put the past behind us. What surprised me about my gesture was the genuine emotion that came with it.

The following week, our father died. Even though I hadn't heard back from my sister, I swallowed hard and prayed for the courage to call her. Her number wasn't in the phone book, so I tried directory service. It was unlisted. *Well,* I thought, *I'm off the hook.* But as I went about my day, a nagging thought persisted until I gave in and tried directory service once more—this time for her ex-husband's number out of state. I dialed the number, and to my disappointment, he answered almost immediately. I told him about my father's death and explained why I had called. We talked for some time, and as soon as I hung up, I dialed the number he had given me. I knew if I didn't, I would find an excuse to put it off, tormenting myself further. I prayed she wouldn't answer.

She picked up after the first ring. "Hello," she said in a familiar voice.

I told her about Daddy. "I finally made it to the post office this morning," she replied, "and I just read your note." We discussed our grievances with amazing courtesy and composure. We talked and cried and forgave. When I hung up, I felt an astonishing sense of healing. My sister later confided she had felt it, too.

The following week, my two sisters, my brother, and I reunited to say goodbye to our parents, our mother having passed away several years earlier. Before we left the cemetery, I had the opportunity to share a verse that God had given me shortly before Daddy's death: "But for you who fear my name, the Sun of Righteousness will rise with healing in his wings. And you will go free, leaping with joy like calves let out to pasture" (Malachi 4:2). A few days later, I received a note from my sister. She wrote to tell me that she felt like one of my calves leaping in the sunlight.

—*Barbara Kugle*

Giving It
All Away

For God has not given us a spirit of fear and
timidity, but of power, love, and self-discipline.

2 Timothy 1:7

The Los Angeles air felt like a heavy sweater pressing against my body as I trudged from the student dining hall to my New Testament living class. Every time I tried to take a deep breath, I coughed, the smog sticking to the inside of my lungs. "I'm here, Lord," I whispered as I chugged up a steep hill. "You promised you'd take care of me, remember?"

God had answered my prayers many times before. After my mother died of cancer, over a year earlier, God's intervention had been clear. I feared I would be stuck in New Jersey forever, unable to finish my undergraduate degree, since I had no money and no way to return to California. Then a relative generously offered to pay for my return ticket. Instead of having to reapply to return to school, I received a housing form with a fifty-dollar deposit as the only requirement for my return.

At the time, it was so easy to see God's hand in my life. Now, with graduation two weeks away, my life was once again at loose ends. My student housing and campus job would end after graduation. I needed to find work and an off-campus apartment quickly. A tap on my right shoulder pulled me from my worried thoughts.

"How's it going?" My friend Cindy said, her blue eyes clouded with worry as she cradled her heavy load of books. "I called you as I came out of the library, but you didn't hear. It was like you were miles away."

I sighed. "I was. Graduation is only two weeks away. I have to find a job and an apartment, and—"

Cindy motioned me toward a nearby bench. "That's better!" she said, dropping her books on the bench. "My term paper for Biblical scholarship has sure required a lot of research."

She caught her breath as I sat beside her, my thoughts still whirling. "Okay," she said. "This isn't like you at all. You're so anxious; it's like you're being eaten up by fear."

"I guess I am," I replied. "But what can do? I've prayed and prayed."

"Remember how God came through for you after your mother died? What did you do then?"

"Well, I waited for God to help me. I got ready every day to come back here, and I just knew He would find a way."

"Why don't you do that now?"

"I have," I said quickly, "but I have to find a job and an apartment or I'll be homeless. I've gone to at least a hundred interviews, and nothing has panned out."

Cindy nodded. "I see the difference."

"You do?"

"Sure. Last time you were confident you were coming back here to finish your degree. And you did! Just do the same thing now."

"But last time, God heard me, and my family helped me. This is different."

"We've got to get to class," she said. "Relax and think about it. You'll figure out what to do. Remember, it's not entirely up to you."

Even though I took Cindy's advice, my fears grew as graduation loomed nearer. I went through my days trying to behave as if I had a job and a place to live after graduation. I applied for every job I could and looked at dozens of apartments. "How can it not be all up to me?" I said as I ate my lunch in the student center. It was four days before graduation.

My friend Jay set his tray on the table across from mine and slid his glasses down his freckled nose to wink at me. "What's up?" he said and grinned.

"You're in a good mood," I said in a voice full of sarcasm.

"I am!" He scooped a huge bite of mashed potatoes with his fork, sighing with pleasure as he chewed. "I sure will miss having the kitchen staff to cook for me after graduation."

"Have you found a place to stay yet?" I asked, anxiety making my voice tight.

"I sure did. I'll be working downtown for a big firm, troubleshooting their software. I even found an apartment within walking distance."

I sighed and twirled my fork in my pile of green beans. "That's just great."

"Your enthusiasm isn't exactly overflowing," Jay said. "What's wrong?"

So, once again, I poured out my worries. My fear had blossomed into outright terror since I'd talked to Cindy. How could I not panic? There were only four days left.

"Don't worry," Jay said and gave my hand a squeeze. "It'll work out. It has to. God is on your side!"

After Jay left, I couldn't help but wonder. "God, you said You'd take care of my needs. Where are You?"

As I studied in the library later that day, I realized that maybe I'd been seeing my situation backwards. After all, God had provided for my physical needs last time. Maybe this time His deliverance would come from the opposite direction. I found a quiet spot in the camellia garden beside the library and bowed my head. "God," I said, lifting my gaze to the sky, "I send my fears about finding a job and a place to stay to You. In their place, please give me the courage to move forward."

It was so simple. It took less than a minute. But afterward, the smoggy air didn't seem so heavy. In fact, I could breathe for the first time in weeks. The next morning as I ate breakfast in the student center, I heard the receptionist announce that I had a phone call.

"Hello, Kriss," a warm female voice said. "We've been trying to reach you. We'd like you to start working for us a week from Monday, if that would be all right."

I blinked hard, going over her words in my head to make sure I'd heard correctly.

"Kriss?" the woman prompted.

"That would be a great time for me to start working for you. Thank you!"

I had just returned to my table to finish my breakfast when my friends Cindy and Linda sat down on either side of me. "We've been looking all over for you," Linda said. "We didn't know if you wanted roommates, or if two roommates would be too many, but we found this great three-bedroom apartment. If we split the rent evenly, it would be a great deal."

"This is unbelievable," I said and told them about the job offer I'd just received.

"I told you it would work out," Cindy said. "Best of all, we get to be roommates."

I wiped away a few tears as I silently thanked God for keeping His promise to care for me. It was then I realized, if he had answered my prayers regarding my physical needs immediately, I wouldn't have learned to give Him the source of all my real problems.

"Well, what do you know?" I murmured. "My fears turned out to be a gift. Thank you, Lord, for accepting them."

—*Kriss Erickson*

From Russia
with Love

*Just think how much more the blood of Christ
will purify our consciences from sinful deeds so
that we can worship the living God. For by the
power of the eternal Spirit, Christ offered himself to God as a perfect sacrifice for our sins.*

Hebrews 9:14

I was terrified that morning. I was about to embark on a mission to tell people about the love of Jesus, but not in my hometown of Portland, Oregon. I was in Tula, Russia, a city of 1 million people. Our group had flown in to Moscow on Thursday evening, and on Saturday, we took the bus down to Tula. It was still winter in Russia, even though the calendar said March. There was snow everywhere, and as I stared out the bus window, I wondered if we would be warm enough. I also wondered, for the umpteenth time, what on Earth I was doing.

I was a stay-at-home mom with three young children, but here I was, thousands of miles from my family. During a meeting at my church, someone said, "Come to Russia by faith. Ninety percent of ministry is just showing up." I had always wanted to obey the Lord in all things, so I decided to show up. Now, I was terrified. Would God show up, too?

The hotel in Tula was old and shabby, but the heat worked. We had lunch in the basement restaurant and then walked back upstairs to meet our interpreters. I prayed my interpreter would be a woman. I prayed she would speak English well. When they assigned me a Christian college student named Natasha, my heart stopped racing—for the moment. Natasha and I began visiting and getting to know one another. It was a huge blessing when we bonded immediately.

The next morning, the group leader used a map to show us the apartment house we would be visiting. Hundreds of concrete blocks of apartments, built during the Stalin era, checkered the city. Our plan was to walk to the top of each block of flats and work our way down, knocking on each apartment door in the hope we would catch people at home during the day.

It was easy for me to see that Natasha shared my anxieties. At breakfast we prayed together, and I asked her to look up Hebrews 9:14. "Just in case," I said.

She opened her Bible, found the verse, and read it to me. "Just think how much more the blood of Christ will purify our consciences from sinful deeds so that we can worship the living God. For by the power of the eternal Spirit, Christ offered himself to God as a perfect sacrifice for our sins."

"Why did you pick that verse?" she asked.

"We might meet someone who is struggling with a guilty conscience. The blood of Jesus cleanses us from all sin, first and foremost, but it also purifies the conscience. There are people who desperately need to know that."

While Natasha meditated on Hebrews 9:14, I prayed to express my willingness to trust the Lord in everything He wanted to do that day—despite my growing fears. It was my natural inclination to depend on myself, but that day, more than anything, I wanted God to show me which path to take. "Lord, I'm trusting in you," I said. "With all my heart."

We started knocking on doors about 9:30 that morning. By the time we reached the second story, it was almost time for lunch. "Shall we go back to the hotel now?" Natasha asked in a hopeful voice.

"Sounds good to me." I was just as eager to take a break as she was. "But we're almost done with this floor. Let's try one more door." I had no way of knowing that God was about to work in a wonderful way.

I knocked on the door of the apartment, and an elderly woman came out in the hallway. She introduced herself as Maria. I'm just over five feet tall, and Maria's head barely reached my shoulder. She took one look at me and said, "God sent you."

I asked Maria, through my interpreter, if she ever thought about spiritual things. Her answer surprised me. "All the time," she said.

When I began to talk to her about the love of God and how sin had separated us all from God, she started to weep. "I know all about that. I committed a great sin when I was a young woman. God will never forgive me." I opened my mouth to speak, but Maria held up her hand. "I cannot even tell you. My sin was too terrible. So horrible that I cannot expect forgiveness."

Stunned, I reached out and grabbed Natasha's arm. Maria didn't know me. What on Earth possessed her to divulge this intensely personal information to a total stranger? She had to be at least eighty years old. This would mean that the sin she spoke of must have taken place more than fifty years ago. I couldn't begin to imagine the burden of guilt she had carried for so many years. I told her what the Bible said in Hebrews . . . that the blood of Jesus purifies the conscience. I explained how it wouldn't do us much good to have the sin removed if the guilt remained. It's the guilt that destroys us, and this woman had been wracked with guilt longer than I had been alive.

She kept insisting God could never forgive her, and I kept insisting He could, He would, and He had. Just when I thought I wasn't getting anywhere, her stubbornness melted. It was as if a light bulb clicked on. She threw her arms around me and began to hug me. She hugged me again and again, and then she hugged Natasha. She was so excited, and I was thrilled beyond words, too. Natasha and I had shown up, and God had shown up, too.

That night, Maria came to the place where we conducted our evening meetings. The police had evicted us from the hall we had rented, and they had blocked the streets so cars could not approach or park nearby. It was very cold that March night, and there were piles of snow all around. We were having our meeting outside the building, but a lot people were present, even though they had been forced to walk. Maria came over from her apartment building, and her face was blue from the cold. She was still rejoicing. "I feel so light, I could fly," she said. I smiled and nodded because I knew that the crushing weight of fifty years of guilt had been lifted at last.

—*Molly Smith*

The Pieces
of My Life

The blessing of the Lord makes a person rich,
and he adds no sorrow with it.

Proverbs 10:22

After thirty years of marriage, I suddenly found myself alone and homeless. As if that wasn't enough, a month later, my employer of fifteen years announced they were moving their television manufacturing operation overseas. The plant would close in six months. While I succumbed to grief and shock, other believers lifted me in prayer. Only groanings came from my heart when I prayed for myself during these trying circumstances.

Where was I going to find work at the age of fifty? And a place to live that I could afford? I recalled an old expression, "what doesn't kill you makes you stronger," so I combed through the classifieds every day and sent out my resume. In the evenings, I pored over scripture to find the strength and guidance I lacked.

The affordable rentals I looked at were in major disrepair or located in unsafe neighborhoods. I called a Realtor who listened politely as I poured out my woes. "Could I still qualify to buy a house?" I asked.

"Sure. How much could you pay down on it?" she asked.

"I only have $500," I replied.

She coughed, or was it a smothered laugh? "Well, I don't know about that, but I'll call you if something turns up."

I wondered if I would ever hear from her again. I had forgotten that the Lord, who multiplied a small boy's lunch of biscuits and fishes to feed five thousand people, was on my side. Several days later the Realtor called. "Would you like to look at a few houses this afternoon?"

The first two houses she showed me were awful, but the third, a small, white Cape Cod, was appealing. She unlatched the "lockbox" with her key and opened the front door. The renter's large friendly dog greeted us, but he had done what dogs do when they're shut up all day. The stench was overwhelming. I covered my nose, determined to concentrate on the house's structure and possibilities. Right away, I knew this was the house for me.

The seller's price was $46,000, a lot of money for an old house in 1984. Back outside, I asked the Realtor all kinds of questions. Then, with uncharacteristic boldness, I made an offer of $36,000 and began to list my stipulations. The house would have to be fumigated, the carpet replaced, a dryer hookup installed, and the ragged wiring and panel box upgraded to city code. The Realtor's eyes widened with each condition I stated. I went on to request that the seller pay all closing costs, since I had only $500. When I finished, the Realtor burst out laughing.

"You've got to be kidding," she said. However, she produced the necessary forms, and using the hood of her car, she wrote up my offer—still laughing.

"I know I'm asking a lot," I said, "but what have I got to lose? Besides, God owns the gold and silver in every mine, and if it's in His will for me, He'll make it all work out." The Realtor rolled her eyes and gathered up her papers. Wearing a big grin, she told me she would call when she knew anything.

My enthusiasm waned as the days went by, but a week after I made my offer, the Realtor called. She wouldn't say anything over the phone, and she asked me to stop by and see her after work. When

I opened her office door, her first comment was, "You're not going to believe what I'm about to tell you." This time she wasn't laughing. Instead, her voice resounded with awe as she explained that the sellers had indeed accepted my offer on the house, including all my terms. Other prospective buyers, it seemed, had been reluctant to look inside once they encountered the terrible smell. The sellers were desperate to sell the property, which belonged to their son who was heavily in debt.

Proverbs 10:22 says, "The blessing of the Lord makes a person rich, and he adds no sorrow with it." God blessed me by multiplying my $500 and diminishing my sorrow at the same time. At the closing, He also showed me that He had a sense of humor when the filing fees, stamps, and deed search came to a total of $502.36. As we left the loan office, the Realtor told me she admired my faith. "Only God could have caused the seller's circumstances to coincide with your needs and work out this deal for you," she said and then added, "Your mortgage payment will be a third of what the renters were paying."

My employer had a good dental plan, so I decided to have a thorough checkup before my job ended. At my appointment, I discovered that the office manager was planning to retire, so I told the dentist I would soon be in need of work, and emphasized that

I was skilled in office work. We set up an interview. He offered me the job, and his manager agreed to stay on until my current job officially ended.

I have learned that nothing happens by chance. God is in control, even in the bad times, and He has a plan for each one of His children. I love to imagine Him moving the pieces of my life around like a puzzle until they fit His plan for me exactly. Sometimes, the circumstances that knock me down are the same ones that drive me to my knees, resulting in a closer relationship with God. I know His promises are true. When the pieces of my life fall into place, it is the blessing of the Lord, and He wants to bless me today. I can trust Him with all the pieces of my life.

—*Imogene Johnson*

A Different Kind
of Jonah Story

Take delight in the Lord,
and he will give you your heart's desires.

Psalm 37:4

You're probably familiar with the story of Jonah from the book of Genesis. Well, my Jonah story also originates in the Bible, but it comes from the book of Psalms—Psalm 37:4 to be exact. I first read the verse early one morning as I stole a little quiet time away from my three kids and husband. *Cool!* I thought. *If I want something God will give it to me.* As I spent more time meditating on the words, I realized they didn't refer to the longings of *my* heart. Instead, God had promised to give me a desire for the same things He wanted for me. That was even better.

I decided to pray the verse as an open invitation to God. For thirty days I prayed, "Lord, whatever this desire is, I invite you to place it on my heart. Inspire me to share it with you and to want it more than I've ever wanted anything before." He was faithful to answer my prayer, but not by causing me to want something. Instead, He showed me how much He had already given me. Suddenly, I saw my life like an outsider looking in. My husband, David, and I both worked at jobs we enjoyed. We had three bright, beautiful, and healthy children, lived in a safe community with excellent public schools, belonged to a loving church family, and enjoyed the love and encouragement of our extended families and neighbors.

At the time, I was working on an article about the many ways families paid for college. I had gone to great lengths to find families from around the country in a variety of socioeconomic situations, but as my interviews progressed, I was surprised to realize my subjects all had one thing in common. Without exception, they had adopted some or all of their children. I asked a few questions about the adoptions just to be polite, but I didn't need the information for my article, so I soon forgot it. Or, at least I tried to. That's when a funny thing happened.

I started encountering adoption everywhere. I would spot a Caucasian couple in the grocery store with an Asian baby, push my cart around the corner, and spot another one. I ran into old friends anxious to tell me all about their recent adoptions. People I had known for years would say out of the blue, "Well, you know I'm adopted." I turned on the radio only to hear a program about adoption. I turned on the television, and there it was again. How in the world was I going to tell my fifty-three-year-old husband that I was pretty sure God wanted us to adopt?

I confided in my friend, Paula, a Christian whose opinion I valued. "Mimi," she said, "God is not in the business of breaking up marriages. Do you really think He would put this on your heart and not David's, too?" She made sense, but I was still scared.

I e-mailed one of the mothers from my article and asked questions about their overseas adoption. I started printing her replies and casually leaving them where David drank his morning coffee. Finally, I mustered the courage to ask him if he had noticed any of the messages. It turned out he loved the idea. I swallowed hard. "Do you think we ought to adopt?"

"Not overseas," he replied. "Why should we spend $40,000 when we could put the money in a college fund and adopt from this country?" I couldn't believe my ears. David had lost his mind, too.

That night, we sat the kids down and told them what we were considering. They went ballistic.

They wanted a baby, and they wanted one now! We explained we'd have to wait until an infant became available. It felt great to finally acknowledge God's desire for me, but in truth, I was scared to death. Surely God was overestimating me. At forty-three, I was already balancing a lot with three kids. I had already started to worry about the day when he might want to meet his birth parents.

We began praying for our baby every morning. We had no way of knowing if he was born yet, or if his mother was pregnant with him, but we prayed for him, for her, and for everyone involved in caring for him. We also prayed we would know how to be the best family possible for him.

Five months later, I picked up the kids from school. I knew they hadn't thought about a thing all day except the fact we were getting their baby brother that evening. The day before, I received a call from an adoption worker. "We have a one-year-old boy entering the system. Do you want him?" *Do we want him?* I thought as my knees buckled. *Do we want him?* What kind of question was that?

"Yes! Yes, we want him." I said and then panicked. "But we don't have a car seat, diapers, clothes, or bottles." Not knowing the age of the child we would be offered, it had been impossible to prepare. We had a crib and high chair. That was it.

"No problem," the worker replied. "The case worker will meet you at Wal-Mart. You can get everything you need there. Tomorrow at four o'clock. Okay?" My legs were mush, my mind was numb, and I hung up without asking a thing about the baby.

The next afternoon, David was stuck in a meeting, so the kids and I made a frantic dash for Wal-Mart, camera in tow, to the diaper aisle where we had agreed to meet. No one was there. We stood and watched every cart that passed. A woman went by with a baby dressed in pink, another with a baby who was too old, and yet another with one too young. Finally, a woman looked at us and waved. In her cart was a tiny boy dressed in camouflage pants and a muscle shirt. He smiled immediately, and when I reached for him, he leapt into my arms.

We brought him home and spent the evening staring at him in amazement. Then, we spent half the night watching him sleep. I recalled Ephesians 3:20—my Jonah verse. "Now all glory to God, who is able, through His mighty power at work within us, to accomplish infinitely more than we might ask or think."

That Sunday, we presented our new son to our church family, and we asked everyone to pray for us. The church threw a baby shower and gave us everything we needed and more. We met his mother and father, but only briefly. They were young and didn't have the resources to give him a good life, but they loved him enough to find someone who could. God loved me enough to let me be that someone.

That was four years ago. Jonah has grown into a lively and delightful kindergartener, and we can't imagine what our lives would be like without him. He has never met a bug, a frog, a puddle, or a tractor he didn't love. Two months ago, he asked me to explain how he could invite Jesus into his heart. I did, and the following Sunday, our church family offered praise and thanksgiving as we watched his baptism. That night, the sunset was particularly spectacular. "Hey, look!" he said. "I think God did that because He's proud of me for inviting Jesus into my heart."

The next morning he engaged in his favorite pastime—climbing way too high in a tree and scaring me half to death. I called up to him. "Oh, look at that cute little squirrel climbing Mommy's magnolia tree."

"No, Mom," he said in his silliest voice. "I'm not a squirrel. I'm your little gift from God, remember?"

I suppose that says it all.

—*Mimi Greenwood Knight*

A Closet Full
of Holes

*Don't copy the behavior and customs of this
world, but let God transform you into a new
person by changing the way you think. Then
you will learn to know God's will for you,
which is good and pleasing and perfect.*

Romans 12:2

As I dragged the shipping box across the wet
floor, the bitterly cold winds chilled me to the
bone. The container weighed more than 300 pounds.
The icy snow dripping from my heavy work boots
made the cargo floor extremely slippery, and my feet
started to give way beneath me as I strained to get the
massive load to the open cargo door of the 727 jet. It
was well after midnight. The storm had kept all flights
circling the black winter night sky for quite some time,

with weary passengers anxious to land, which meant even more work for me ahead. My tired body ached from the physical strain and the bitter cold.

As I struggled to get the box on the turning belt loader, my hands felt numb in my gloves because I had been out in the cold so long. A person passing by would not have known that I was handling the pressure of the cold and the massive job of unloading a full 727 by the grace of God. It had taken me over a year to get to the point of working in His grace while under pressure.

For many years, I had a volatile temper, at times almost uncontrollable. My father had a similar temper and unknowingly mentored and molded me into the young man I had become. When things didn't go my way I would explode. In high school football, this was an asset, but in a marriage, it was proving to be destructive.

I had accepted Jesus as my Savior some years earlier. Some bad habits dropped off more quickly than others. My pipe and cigar smoking, which I had picked up in the military, seemed to let go almost without a fight. The temper and cursing was a different story. They had rooted themselves so deeply that they were a part of me.

One evening, I was working the sound booth at our church when something went wrong with the equipment I was using. Expletives shot from my mouth like flames within seconds without me even realizing it. Fortunately, no one was around to hear me, but it was then I realized my sin was rooted deeper in bondage than I had previously thought.

I began a quest to destroy the deep-seated problem before it damaged not only me personally, but also my testimony to others. I decided to comb through a concordance to find everything God had to say about anger, self-control, and using God's name in vain. As I spent countless hours reading, writing, and memorizing scriptures, I began to feel a process of renewal emerge from within me.

I had hoped the process would be quick and painless, but I finally realized that the anger and cursing had been building for a long time, and its evil roots would not quickly shrivel up and die without a fight.

Little by little, my attitude began to change, as God's word became more and more a part of me. I discovered that when I gave full vent to my anger, I was not macho, as I once thought. According to the Bible, I was a fool. God said that a wise man keeps himself under control—a God-given control. I learned that it's better to control my temper than to control a whole city.

Slowly, these truths lifted me out of the miry pit of uncontrolled anger, and I felt some control returning to my life. I even started dropping my guard and began to think I could control the anger by myself.

That is, until my wife asked me to lower our young kids' closet pole so they could learn to hang up their clothes. It was a hot summer day, and I was hard at work in their tight little closet. I was about to put up the newly cut pole when I discovered I had cut the pole just a few inches short and it would not fit in the closet mounts. For some reason this set off a chain of anger that left the inside of that closet looking like the aftermath of World War III. I took that pole and began pounding the inside of the closet. Over and over, I pounded holes in the drywall.

When I finished, I was exhausted and ashamed for choosing to descend into that miry stinking pit of uncontrolled anger. My first thought was to patch up the holes so no one would know, but God had a different idea. He impressed me to leave the holes, and whenever I thought "I" could control my anger, I could open the closet and see how close I was to losing it. Until we sold our house years later, at which time I repaired the holes, the kids had a "holy" closet, and I had a visual reminder that it was God's control, not mine, that gives me victory.

However, it was on that bitter cold winter night while loading freight that I truly experienced God's transforming power over my anger. I had turned the belt loader on in anticipation of putting the cargo on it. Then, stopping the loader, I would go to the bottom and take the items off and put them into the freight carts. The 300-pound box was giving me a big problem. It was creating a lot of resistance, even on the slippery floor. I pulled on it with a jerk, and when I slipped, the box landed on my freezing hand, trapping it with the belt loader grinding away at my hand.

This was the moment, where by God's grace, Romans 12:2 became a reality for me. I was miraculously able to pull my smashed hand from under the casket, and instantly, I shouted, "Praise the Lord, I didn't hurt it worse." There was no kicking the casket and screaming curses. There was only praise for my creator. I wasn't trying to impress anyone; there was no one around. I was still cold, my hand still hurt, and the plane still needed to be unloaded, but I knew I had let God transform me into a new person by changing the way I thought. God's Word had replaced the evil roots, and I was no longer conformed to the world's image of an angry, macho, cursing man.

I still get angry thoughts, but I no longer act upon them. As I walk further and further into the light of the Lord's truth, my former self has become a shriveled shadow. Now, it seems strange talking about the "old" me. It took a closet full of holes and a near tragic accident to bring me face to face with the fact that only God's power can bring death to our old self and give birth to the new.

—*Don Sultz*

Angels on
the Tailpipe

God is our refuge and strength,
always ready to help in times of trouble.

Psalm 46:1

When I answered the phone, I heard my son Jon's faltering voice. "Mom? Mom, I'm so sorry." He sounded distant, strained, and afraid. He was supposed to be at an interview for a summer job. My heart began to race.

"What are you talking about?" I asked. "Are you in Florence?"

I heard muffled voices in the background. "Here, I'd better let someone else explain," he said.

An elderly woman's voice came on the line. "Hello. My husband and I were following your son down Highway 101 when his car started to drift across the road. It looked like he fell asleep at the wheel. He's lucky he landed where he did. Another fifty feet and he would have been over the edge. We've called the paramedics, and they should be here soon."

I began to panic. "Where are you?"

"We're just outside of Florence," the woman replied, "and he's still climbing out of the air bag. The car's a mess. He's got a bump on his head, and I think he's in shock. They'll probably take him to the hospital." There was silence, followed by more muffled voices.

"Mom?" My son came on the line again. "I'm so sorry."

"Please tell me you're all right."

"The state police just arrived. I've got to go."

The line went dead. I tried redial, but I didn't get an answer. Tears filled my eyes as I called my husband Loren at work. "You've got to come home," I said. "Jon's been in an accident on the coast highway."

Jon had moved to Newport, Oregon, at the end of March 2006 to spend the spring term in an ocean studies class at Hatfield Marine Science Center, an arm of the biology program at Oregon State University. We loaned him a car to use since the apartments where he would live at the science center were on the south end of the bridge that spanned Yaquina Bay, and Newport's business district was on the north end. Jon liked being able to go to church and get his own groceries while living at Hatfield, something he couldn't have done without the car.

As the term progressed, he applied for summer job opportunities. Today had been one of those interviews: a job in Florence, fifty miles south of his apartment. He had called that morning, and we had prayed for traveling mercies for him. He admitted he was nervous since he would be driving an unfamiliar span of highway. I reminded him that God promised to never leave us nor forsake us. "For I will be with you as I was with Moses. I will not fail you or abandon you" (Joshua 1:5).

Throughout the morning, I prayed for Jon. When I realized enough time had passed for him to make the interview I stopped, never imagining that something life-threatening would soon transpire.

Now, the time began to pass in a blur. Loren came home and gathered necessary documents to reclaim the car as well as insurance papers for both Jon and the vehicle. Since the pickup my husband drove only seated two, I agreed I should stay home in order for Loren to take Jon back to Newport the next day. It was a difficult decision; I wanted to see my son.

I called the science center and told them about the accident so they wouldn't worry about Jon. I also reached the agency where Jon was to have interviewed and let them know. Everyone was relieved that nothing serious had happened to him. One young woman in Jon's biology program called back for details so she could relay the information to the others enrolled at Newport. I settled back in my chair to pray, all the while wondering if God had heard my petitions that morning. If so, why had this happened? Over and over in my mind I could still hear the words of the woman at the scene of the accident. "Another fifty feet and he would have been over the edge."

The scenery along the Pacific Coast is known for its rugged beauty. Like a piece of unruly ribbon, the highway twists and turns, falling into shadow as trees spring up, then bursting into sun with wide spans of the ocean beyond. Cars have been known to go off the road, and I shuddered to think what might have happened had Jon fallen asleep at the edge of a precipice, with nothing but a guardrail to prevent him from dropping into the churning surf. I found myself in tears over and over again that afternoon, as the enormity of what had happened played itself out in my mind.

The phone rang again mid-afternoon. "Mom, I'm at the Florence hospital," Jon said. "They checked me out and said I could go home."

"Dad's on his way to pick you up," I replied. "In fact, he should be there soon."

Later, I learned that when my husband entered the emergency department, the state policeman who had appeared at the scene met him. "Your son was very fortunate," the officer said. "If he had drifted the other way, he might have landed in the ocean. Or, if a car had been coming in the opposite lane, he might have had a head-on collision."

With the hospital's bill settled, and the title to the car transferred to the wrecking company, Loren and Jon traveled north to return Jon to his apartment. Two weeks remained in the term, so Loren filled the refrigerator and pantry before he left for home, but we all we resigned ourselves to the fact that Jon would be unable to drive to church. We were in for more blessings. Other students offered Jon rides to the grocery store, and one of the janitors at the science center made a special point of getting up on Sunday and dropping Jon at church, even though he didn't attend himself.

When my husband returned home the following afternoon, he told me what he had seen at the accident site. Crossing a lane of traffic, Jon had hit a curve in the road where an embankment broke his drift. If he had traveled further up the highway the incline could have tilted the car toward the ocean and possibly sent him over the edge. Instead, the car gently slid into a ditch on its left side, as if a giant hand had grasped the tailpipe and guided the car to its resting place. Obviously, God and his angels had been with our son throughout the accident. Jon received a small bump on his forehead that didn't even bruise.

I praised God for the outcome. He kept His promise from Psalm 46 on what could have been a fatal day. As He had so many times before, the Lord answered my prayers in His own time and in His own way. What more could I ask for?

—*Patricia Lee*

Quail and
Manna

How precious is your unfailing love, O God!
All humanity finds shelter
in the shadow of your wings.
You feed them from the abun-
dance of your own house,
letting them drink from your river of delights.

Psalm 36:7-8

I wandered aimlessly around my kitchen, peering into the dark abyss of the pantry and poking around the few containers in the refrigerator. Despite my hunt for food, the sad state of affairs remained the same. There was nothing in the house to eat.

True, I wasn't starving, but as I walked by the hallway mirror, I could tell, even through my fluffy pink robe with black dogs embroidered on the lapel, that I was losing more weight in addition to the pounds that had evaporated under stress. It was another pathetic ingredient to add to the feast of my pity party.

The year 2008 was about to be written off as a very bad, terrible, awful year, and it was only February. The autumn of 2007 had given a jump-start to the descent of my existence. My firstborn had flown the coop; never mind that she was living on campus at a Christian college twenty minutes away and majoring in nursing. My husband of twenty-nine years moved out two months later, leaving my eleven-year-old daughter, Lydia, and I to fend for ourselves. In January, a mass was found in my colon, and in February, I had surgery for colon cancer.

Now at home two weeks later, I still couldn't even sit up straight because of four angry incisions. Driving a car was out of the question, so I was homebound and feeling the crazy effects of cabin fever. I was trying to engage in all the right godly activities: praying, reading my Bible, singing praise songs, and meditating. After days of eating ice chips in the hospital, I was in no mood to add fasting to my list of pious deeds.

Friends from church had showered us with cans of soup and frozen TV dinners, but we had almost polished off the donated food, and besides,

I was just plain hungry for meat. Finally, I plopped myself down in a chair by the fireplace and read the Bible.

Suddenly, I heard my front door open. I panicked, partly because I looked frightful and partly because Lydia was at her grandma's house, and I knew it couldn't be her. I peeked around the corner to see Jake, a classmate of Lydia's, carry a large container to my kitchen. "Jake, what have you got there? You nearly scared me to death."

"My mom went to a health food store to get us some chicken for supper," he replied. "She thought you probably would like one, too. It's fully cooked and still warm. I hope you can eat solid food now."

After he left, I stared at the nicely browned chicken roosting on my counter. Somebody might as well have dropped the crown jewels in my lap. That poultry looked so beautiful, it could have been a smorgasbord centerpiece. The aroma was overwhelming, so I yanked a fork out of the silverware drawer and dug in. It was too late for lunch and too early for supper, but I ate and plucked meat and skin from the bone until I was silly.

After about half an hour of carnivorous activity, I lounged on the couch like a stuffed turkey. I was sincerely grateful, but the only thing I could think about was how badly I wanted some bread. "God," I said, "You know that, for the most part, I am a woman who could live on carbohydrates alone, but there isn't one slice of bread or stale bun in the house. Why did they have to relocate the bakery? I would have walked there myself, even in my dilapidated condition."

Just as I was about to sink into a whole different pit of depression, the doorbell rang. *How strange,* I thought. *I haven't had two visitors in two weeks and I get two in one day.* When I opened the door, a woman from my church was standing on the porch. Sharon and I had been friends as teenagers, but we hadn't talked in years.

"I was baking some bread from my mother-in-law's recipe, and I was thinking about you and everything you've been through this year," she said. "I don't know if you like thick, wheat bread, but I felt like I should make an extra loaf for you."

My eyes filled with tears as I took it from her hands. Only God would know she had brought me my favorite bread in the whole world. I told Sharon about my afternoon's craving and what my resulting experiences had been. As the sun went down, we sat and talked until we had caught up on several years' worth of living. We talked about the goodness of God and how often He worked through His Church and His people.

After hugging Sharon goodbye, I raced back to the kitchen. With a giant knife, I attacked the loaf of bread and dined until I qualified as a human breadbox. Now, I was a stuffed turkey, complete with dressing. As I wandered around my house, no longer aimlessly, delight, satisfaction, and contentment coursed through my veins.

Counting my blessings and remembering how God had been so faithful to me in the past, gave me a renewed energy and hope. Being a well-fed woman didn't hurt, either. I now had the energy to believe that God would provide a home for Lydia and me in the coming months. Maybe He would be so generous as to drop a job on my front steps someday soon, too. If not, He would use His people, the members of my church to meet my needs.

In forty-some years of being a Christian, I have witnessed God perform incredible deeds. I have seen Him repeatedly prove Himself to be faithful and true to me personally and to believers around me. The more I read His promises from His Word, the more I believe they are reliable guarantees. However, the most precious part of His love comes from knowing that His love and faithfulness are not dependent on my faithfulness. He gives freely to overflowing—just because He wants to. He loves His children that much.

—*Evangeline Ruth Beals*

O, Ye of
Little Faith

Seek the Kingdom of God above all else, and
live righteously, and he will give you every-
thing you need. So don't worry about tomor-
row, for tomorrow will bring its own worries.
Today's trouble is enough for today.

Matthew 6:33–34

I don't know why I had so little faith. I believed in
God, and I loved the Lord Jesus. I went to church,
read my Bible, and prayed. But I was a worrier, and a
few years ago, my number one worry was retirement.
How would I be able to afford it with no savings and
no retirement fund? What would I do about rent,
food, clothing, and other living expenses? For years,
I had lived from paycheck to paycheck, barely able to
make ends meet on my salary as a secretary.

It looked like I might have the opportunity to afford retirement, after all, when I went to work for an aircraft company in Seattle, Washington. It was my last full-time job of a nearly thirty-year working career. In my late fifties at the time, I planned to stay with the company until I turned seventy, when I would become eligible for their pension.

A year and a half later, my mother became ill and could no longer live alone at her home in California. She wanted to come to Washington and stay with me. I wanted to take care of her and make her happy, so I flew to California and brought her home to my apartment south of Seattle.

I hired a "companion"—and paid her more than half my salary—to stay with my mother while I was at work. The cost became prohibitive, and my daughter encouraged us to move south to Olympia, so she could help with the care of my mother. As a result, I had to quit the company, and my plans for working there until I retired at age seventy went out the window, along with that elusive pension.

At the age of sixty-one, I moved to Olympia with my eighty-one year old mother, and we rented a house on a local golf course. I took a part-time job with the state and hired another "mother sitter." My mother loved living on the golf course. She'd sit on the back deck in sunny weather and cheer the golf-ers as they passed by. Sadly, her health worsened, and she passed away just three years later.

My mother left me some money, and I bought a lovely mobile home at a park in nearby Lacey. I lived there for five years, but the trailer pad rent kept going up, as did the cost of upkeep. I worked part-time as a babysitter during this time, but still I found it difficult to make ends meet. All these things provided wonderful additions to my collection of concerns.

One day, my son-in-law brought me an application for a low-income apartment complex for seniors in Olympia. He was the gardener at the facility and reassured me that it was a nice place. Around the same time, I learned that a friend from my church lived in one of the apartments. I paid her a visit and was pleasantly surprised by her lovely home and the beautiful grounds with velvety green lawns. I immediately applied for an apartment and was disheartened to discover a two-year waiting list. Once again, I worried. How could I hold on that long in my dire financial situation? However, this time, I stopped fretting long enough to pray.

After a few short months, I received a call from the manager of the apartment complex. "I have an apartment for you," she said. "You can move in a month."

Her call caught me off guard. I told her I hadn't put my mobile home on the market yet. "That's all right," she said. "You can turn it down once, if you're not ready, and still remain at the top of the list."

I promptly put my home up for sale. When a month went by with no action, I had to turn down the apartment, but a short while later, a couple made an offer, and I accepted. We arranged for a one-month escrow. As usual, my anxieties surfaced. What if a month went by, and I had no place to go? Where would I live? What would I do with my two cats? Where would I store my furniture? There seemed to be no end to my worries but, once more, I took the time to pray.

Imagine my amazement when, the very next day, the apartment manager called and said, "We have another apartment for you, and it will be ready in a month."

I was ecstatic. I praised God and thanked Him for His faithfulness—as well as His perfect timing! And in a still, small voice, He reminded me. "I told you not to worry. Remember the birds of the air and the lilies of the field? I feed them, clothe them, and take care of them. Never forget that I will always take care of you. You are my child, and I love you." From that day on, my faith grew, and as it flourished, my doubts and fears lost their power.

—Gay Sorensen

An Unscheduled
Stop

God is my shield,
saving those whose hearts are true and right.

Psalm 7:10

The scratching sound in our attic sent chills up my spine. The scurrying of little paws overhead triggered frenzied barking in our shih tzu, Maggie. I sent up a frantic flare prayer. While I couldn't see them, I knew the noise had to be squirrels. They are a homeowner's nightmare if trapped inside the attic. Torturous images of ripped insulation, gnawed electrical wires, holes in the sheetrock, and a slew of other damages haunted my thoughts.

I flipped through the yellow pages and located a pest control service. They promised to respond that

afternoon. Jimmy's arrival put my concerns somewhat at ease. He was an amiable young man with
a slow Texas drawl, crystal blue eyes, and a smile as
big as Dallas. "Ma'am," he said, "you've got squirrels
in your attic. Unless we remove them, they'll stay
until the babies can find their way out, or worse."

He climbed the dropdown stairs leading to the
attic in our two-story house and laid traps, but the
squirrels proved too smart to swallow the bait. Time
passed, and more flare prayers went up. When my
furry visitors finally found their way out, Jimmy
removed the traps and boarded up their place of
entry. Blissful peace and quiet returned to our home
once more.

During the squirrel "wars," I became acquainted
with Jimmy. He told me a little of his life story,
which included a bout with alcoholism earlier in
life. His wife at the time also struggled with alcohol
and drug addiction. "One day," he said, "I woke up
knowing if I was ever going to have a chance at staying sober, I'd have to get away from her. I left and
got a divorce. After a spell, I started going to church
and soon gave my heart to the Lord. I've been sober
now for eight years. I met a pretty little churchgoing
gal. We got married, and have two girls." When he
spoke of teaching his girls about the Lord, his face
beamed.

We finalized our business with the squirrels, and Jimmy inquired about ongoing pest control service. He recommended a quarterly maintenance plan, and we scheduled his return visit.

A few months later, at the conclusion of my devotionals one morning, I whispered, "Lord, use me for Your glory today." I smiled when I gave more thought to my request, and I realized I had no plans to leave the house and expected no visitors. The day suddenly took on an air of expectancy.

Midmorning, the doorbell rang. A look through the beveled glass revealed Jimmy and another young man—a week early. When I opened the door, Jimmy greeted me. "Mrs. Blagg, I was in the neighborhood today and wondered if I could go ahead and service your property?"

"Sure. Jimmy, come on in."

He turned to introduce his assistant, Daniel. "Morning," Daniel mumbled. He was a tall, olive complexioned young man with piercing brown eyes, and coarse, black hair that brushed his shoulders. His shy, soft-spoken demeanor masked a melancholy air about him.

Jimmy explained that Daniel would service the exterior of our house and yard while he handled the interior. After delivering final instructions to Daniel, he stepped inside and closed the door. As he removed his shoes, his usual custom before beginning work inside, he offered a brief history of his relationship with Daniel.

"Remember when I told you about my first marriage? Daniel is my first wife's son by another marriage. I'm the closest thing he's ever had to a real father. The hardest thing about leaving her was leaving Daniel. I love that kid." Jimmy assembled his equipment and continued. "One night, a couple of weeks ago, he showed up on my doorstep. Said he needed a place to sleep. He's been sleeping on our couch ever since. I've been showing him the ropes of the business and hired him as my helper through the summer. He's been living in north Texas with his mother. A few months ago, she walked out and nobody's seen her since. He had no place else to go."

"He seemed rather somber and sad," I replied.

"He's been hitchhiking to the state pen in Huntsville every week to see his real dad, who's serving a life sentence plus ninety-nine years for murder. Last week we were in the truck driving to a job and Daniel broke down crying. He feels like he has no one." As he climbed the stairs, Jimmy pulled a rumpled handkerchief from his pocket and wiped his eyes. It was obvious his concern for Daniel weighed heavy on his heart.

Whispering a prayer for Daniel, I wondered what I could do to pump life and encouragement into this precious young man. Then I remembered a book in my library that gave the Biblical meaning of a person's name. After a quick search of my shelves, I found it. I whisked through its pages and located Daniel's name. Retrieving a note card from my desk, I wrote out a passage from Jeremiah 29.

After the two completed their work, we gathered in the kitchen while Jimmy wrote out the invoice. I took two cold bottles of water from the fridge and I handed one to Daniel. "You have a Biblical name," I said to him and smiled. "Do you know what it means?"

"No, ma'am," he replied.

"In Biblical days, Hebrew parents gave their sons and daughters names that reflected the character traits they wanted instilled in the children's lives. Whenever the child heard their name, they heard the character trait his name implied. The parents sought to remind their children that they were unique and had great worth in the sight of God. Daniel means, 'God is my judge.' God wants you to know that His thoughts toward you take precedence over all others. A scripture verse for Daniel is found in Psalm 7:10, 'God is my shield, saving those whose hearts are true and right.'"

He lifted his head and looked me in the eye.

"What are your plans after high school?"

He shrugged, "I don't know."

"Daniel, God loves you. He loved you before the world was even created. You are one-of-a-kind in His eyes." I gently took his large, callused hands in mine. "Could I pray with you?" I asked, and he nodded. "Precious Lord, reveal your great love to Daniel. Help him to know You as his loving, heavenly Father. Lead him to discover the unique gifts, skills, and abilities You've placed within him. Lift the despair and loneliness from his heart. Guide him to know that he's never alone, because You are as close as the whisper of Your Name. We ask these things in Jesus' name."

I looked up to see a sparkle in Daniel's eyes and a smile to match. Jimmy stood to the side, his eyes glistening with tears. We walked out the front door together. With a grateful heart, I thanked God for His faithfulness, and for giving me the opportunity to be used for His glory. Even on a day when I had no plans to leave the house, God had His plan, and this one began with some pesky squirrels.

—Jeanette Sharp

The Peace
of God

You will keep in perfect peace
all who trust in you,
all whose thoughts are fixed on you!

Isaiah 26:3

I couldn't remember a time when I felt so jumpy and nervous, and with each passing day, it worsened. Ever since the tragic death of my seventeen-year-old stepson, a few months earlier, I had been going through the motions and feeling anything but alive.

My husband and I had two children of our own. Like most mothers, I was the nucleus of our family, the glue that held everyone together, but, lately, it felt as though my grieving family was directing all of their anger at me. This made it even more difficult to cope with my own despair.

One day at work, after hanging up the phone from yet another argument with my husband over something trivial, the thought of ending it all suspended itself in my mind like a dark, sinister cloud. The constant emotional battle had taken its toll. "Dear Lord, I need help," I whispered aloud.

My coworkers in the office pod where I worked had all left for the day, so when I felt a strong hand on my shoulder, I froze. I turned my chair around and came face to face with Jay, my cousin who worked down the hall. In a soft, comforting voice, Jay asked me if I needed some help. He just happened to have the number of a friend—a Christian counselor. "Would you like to call him?" Jay asked.

In the past, my husband and I had always tried to be there for each other, but neither one of us seemed capable of providing comfort. Neither one of us could think clearly. All we knew was unimaginable pain, and the anger over our loss had begun to poison our relationship. I used to wonder how the death of a child could destroy a marriage. I thought the thread of common pain would bring a couple closer together, and their shared grief would build a bridge instead of a wall. Instead, my husband and I often discovered that when one of us wanted to talk, the other one didn't. I worried about upsetting him by bringing up the tragedy, especially if I sensed he was in a good mood. Both of us forgot the vital role of communication in the healing process.

During my first visit with the counselor, Joe, my tears flowed effortlessly as I poured out my torment to a stranger schooled in listening to hearts, but by the second session, I was disappointed. All he did was listen—and I wanted him to fix it. He would nod occasionally, but showed no emotion whatsoever, even while I had tears streaming down my face. He would ask me how something made me feel, but otherwise he stayed silent. Finally, during the third session, he nailed it. "How much time are you spending in the Bible?" he asked.

The Bible? Didn't he hear me say that I was having trouble focusing on anything, especially reading?

"God's Word has tremendous power," he continued. "And, you don't need to read much for it to help you," he added, almost as if he could read my thoughts.

I just told him I felt abandoned by God in my grief. Had he been daydreaming while I've been talking?

"This is what I'd like you to do," he said and then scribbled something down on a piece of paper and handed it to me. "I want you to look up these two scripture verses and memorize them." His eyes met mine. Neither one of us blinked.

Great, I thought. *I'll be doing well if I can understand the verses, much less memorize them.* As soon as I got home, I looked them up and read them out loud, speaking slowly, as if to a child. "Don't worry about anything; instead, pray about everything. Tell God what you need, and thank him for all he has done. Then you will experience God's peace, which exceeds anything we can understand. His peace will guard your hearts and minds as you live in Christ Jesus."

Those two sentences seemed incredibly long to me, and just as I had suspected, I had trouble comprehending them. But when I read them again, breaking them down into bite-sized morsels and meditating on clusters of a few words at a time, a miraculous transformation began to occur. *Don't worry about anything . . . pray about everything . . . His peace will guard your hearts. . . .* After months of turning my back on God, at first from grief and then from resentment, my soul felt as if it were returning home for a much needed rest.

I had been a strong Christian prior to my stepson's death, but between the weight of the grief and my own anger toward God, I had stopped having my quiet time with the Lord. Even though I continued to attend worship services, I knew I was going through the motions there, too.

I continued repeating the verses over and over in my mind, and each time, the words acted as a soothing balm massaged lovingly into my heart. I felt

warm all over, and the jumpiness I had been suffer-
ing from was actually letting up. I copied the verses
down and kept them in plain view, reading them
several times throughout the day. Later, at bedtime,
I whispered them out loud again, and I had my first
night of deep, restful sleep since losing my stepson.

The next morning, as soon as I got out of bed,
I remembered the verses and read them again. Two
major aspects suddenly stood out in my mind: *Pray
about everything* and *thank Him for all he has done.*
Filled with conviction, I dropped to my knees in
prayer. "Father," I said, "forgive me for not being
thankful; thankful You chose to create my stepson
in the first place, thankful for the opportunity to
know him and to love him, thankful that he was
given seventeen years instead of seventeen minutes,
and thankful he did not suffer." *Yes,* I thought, *there
were so many reasons to be thankful.*

I resumed my habit of morning quiet time with
the Lord, and ever so slowly, I began to crawl out
of the deep, dark cave in which my soul had been
choking for so many months. As I continued com-
municating with the Lord, my clarity of thinking
returned. Not only was there a light at the end of the
tunnel; it was getting brighter with each day.

I had been trying to make sense out of a senseless
tragedy, but I finally concluded I would *never* be able

to make any sense out of it. I could only accept it, grow from it, and learn from it. What I have learned has changed my life.

I have learned not to spare hugs. I have learned to be the first one to smile and to share my words of encouragement freely. I have learned that three little words can make all the difference: "I love you," and "I am sorry." But the most important lesson I have learned is to pray about *all* things and to trust God with the results. Then, and only then, will the peace that comes from God alone fill my soul.

—*Connie Sturm Cameron*

A Nightmare and
a Dream Come True

*No power in the sky above or in the Earth
below—indeed, nothing in all creation will ever
be able to separate us from the love of God
that is revealed in Christ Jesus our Lord.*

Romans 8:39

It was a shared enthusiasm for animals that helped bring my husband, Tom, and I together, but it was this same passion that almost tore us apart. Tom had maintained a collection of snakes most of his life; just after we met and married, he became interested in keeping venomous species.

Although I took comfort in the fact that he spent a great deal of time preparing for the presence of these snakes in our home, I could never shake the fear that someday he might be the victim of a bite.

Tom's collection grew to include cobras, vipers, and rattlesnakes. They were kept in a restricted area of our basement in double locked cages. He cared for them in a safe and responsible manner. I may have worried about his well-being, but I never feared for my safety, or the safety of our children.

One morning, just before lunch, he went downstairs to feed his snakes. A few moments later, he returned, his arm wrapped in an Ace bandage and blood on his hand. "I've been bitten," he said in a calm voice. His composure unnerved me, and he explained that he was trying to stay relaxed in order to keep his heart rate down and prevent the venom from spreading more rapidly. He asked me to bring him the bite treatment protocol that he had printed several months ago.

The situation turned surreal. *I must be dreaming,* I thought, *or watching a movie.* I wanted someone to press the stop button on the remote control, or pinch me and end my nightmare. I attempted to mimic Tom's cool demeanor but, within minutes, I panicked. When he announced that he was going to drive himself to the hospital, I regained my self-control and dialed 911.

Within minutes, someone from the poison control center phoned, the local rescue squad arrived, and not long after that, a helicopter landed in the field behind our house. Tom insisted that I accompany him to prevent the Ace bandage from being removed; the bandage he was convinced was keeping him alive. He also needed me to be his voice, to tell the people involved the species of snake that had bitten him and the pertinent details of the incident. The effects of the venom included paralysis, and he was worried he would soon be rendered speechless.

I was devastated when the medical personnel informed me that I couldn't ride in the helicopter. I stood and watched it take off and began to pray—a childlike recitation of only five words. "Please don't let Tom die." I repeated my simple plea over and over as if erecting a barrier against the "unthinkables" trying to force themselves into my mind. A neighbor drove me to the hospital. It was a one-hour drive, and I had no idea what shape Tom would be in when I arrived.

The hospital where he had been taken, a huge teaching facility, was undergoing renovations, and we spent many precious minutes trying to locate the emergency room. We finally found the information desk. A chaplain appeared, and I became hysterical. His appearance must surely mean that Tom was critically ill, or perhaps even dead. Eventually, I discovered that he had been taken to the medical respiratory ICU, and I was escorted to a waiting room.

The head toxicologist entered the room and introduced himself. "I'm very optimistic about Tom's progress," he said in a reassuring voice. "Antivenin to treat the bite is on its way from both Miami and New York." He paused and closed his eyes for a moment, as if searching for the right words. "Your husband is now completely paralyzed, but the antivenin should reverse the paralysis. I'm confident that he'll make a complete recovery."

"Can I see him?" I asked.

The doctor shook his head. "The other doctors and nurses are trying to stabilize his condition." He smiled. "I'll keep you posted."

I returned his smile. "I'm so grateful you're here. The nurses told me you're an expert on snakebites."

He held up his hands. "If I'm an expert, it's because God is working through me," he said. "These hands are His tools."

That's all I needed to hear. God was here and He was in charge—the doctor had even confirmed it. My long wait began. Minutes passed like hours, and hours passed like days. The antivenin arrived. I called out to a nurse entering the ICU and asked once again to see Tom. "No," she said. "The doctors and nurses are still very busy. You'd only be in the way."

The head toxicologist returned to the waiting room, but he was not the positive, encouraging man

I had met only hours before. "I've got serious concerns about Tom's condition," he said. "There's a
chance that once we administer the antivenin, his
heart might stop."

I felt dizzy as a surge of panic hit me. I grabbed
the doctor's arm. "That's not what you said when I
first arrived here," I said. He admitted that he'd never
treated the bite of a black Pakistani cobra, a snake
rarely kept in captivity. Only a few people had ever
been bitten. He explained that without the antivenin,
Tom would remain paralyzed indefinitely or die.

I spent six hours in that tiny waiting room. I felt
betrayed by the toxicologist's admission that Tom might
not make it. He had said God was working through
him, but now he was saying that Tom might die. God
had forgotten me. I found myself unable to summon the
warm, secure feeling of His love. All I felt sitting there,
sniffling and sobbing like a small child without a tissue,
was emptiness. Maybe, I thought with a jab of fear, I
had never had any faith at all. Until the moment I
faced the loss of my beloved Tom, it had never really
been tested. I'd always been able to say the words, but
now I had to find the faith to back them up.

At last I was allowed to see Tom. Completely
paralyzed and, unable to breathe on his own, he had
been placed on a ventilator. He could not even open
his eyes. I felt a hand on my shoulder and turned to

find a nurse standing beside me. "Go ahead," she said. "Touch him. Talk to him. He can hear you. He just can't respond right now."

She went back to her station a few feet away, and I reached down and clasped his hand, the one I recalled closing hard and strong around mine whenever he touched me, a hand that now hung limp and lifeless. *Oh God*, I pleaded silently, *please help my Tom—please help me*. I desperately wanted to believe again. I needed to know that God had not deserted me.

I asked God to let Tom squeeze my hand. I bent down and whispered in his ear. "Please, Tom, squeeze my hand. Please show me that you're going to be okay." The seconds passed in a rhythm that matched my pounding heart. I waited and I prayed. More time went by, and then it happened. I felt it. It was barely discernable but it was a squeeze. I prayed again, this time full of happiness and praise. I knew the antivenin had started to work, and Tom was going to be okay. I had it on the best authority. God, Himself, had answered my plea.

When Tom regained his voice the next day, I asked him if he had been frightened.

"No," he said. "Not really."

"But you might have died. Didn't that scare you?"

He shook his head. "At first," he said, "I thought I was staying calm on my own, trying to keep the venom from spreading more quickly. Then I realized that God was right there with me. He was keeping me calm. It was as if He had His hand resting on my head, just to let me know He was there."

I thought about the sign I had prayed for and I nodded. "Yes," I said, "He was most definitely there."

"When I left the ICU," Tom continued, "I had a lot of time to think. I realized that God had a purpose for me. He had saved me for a reason, and I believe He wants us to find a church home. He wants our children to know Jesus."

A few weeks after Tom came home, a car pulled up in our driveway, and two men got out. They introduced themselves as the pastor and assistant pastor of a church about ten miles from our farm. "It's funny," the pastor said, "but we've driven past your place many times and never stopped, but today, I felt a very powerful urge to pull in and invite you to our church."

That was five years ago. As a result of attending church, Tom and I rededicated ourselves to the Lord, and our five children found salvation. Our road is rarely smooth. We still stumble, we still get lost and, sometimes, we may even be plunged into darkness and find ourselves unable to move forward, but God has the road map, and He knows exactly where we're going. Everything is going to be all right.

—*Susan B. Townsend*

Because
They're Mine

For where two or three gather together because
they are mine, I am there among them.

Matthew 18:20

May 22, 2008 was a memorable day. My youngest child, Charlie, was about to graduate kindergarten. I was experiencing a variety of feelings: pride in what a handsome, sweet boy Charlie had become, and sadness over the independence he would gain in moving on to first grade.

"Don't cry," I told myself as I drove the kids to school that morning. I dropped off my twelve-year-old son, Christian, and then, drove Alex and Charlie across town to their school. "Do you have your swimsuits and towels?" I asked my two youngest. They were going to an end-of-school party at their karate studio for the entire afternoon and had invited three friends.

"What if it rains?" Alex asked, looking at the gray sky layered in clouds. "Will we still have the party?"

"I think so," I said. "You'll probably just play inside instead of having water balloon fights."

"That stinks," he said.

"Now listen, Alex. You go straight to karate after school," I said. "Be sure to tell Ellis and Cole to go with you."

"Yes, Mom," he replied in a tone that told me he was far too old for his mother to be giving him orders.

"Charlie and Austin will already be there," I said as we drove up to the school.

"Yes, Mom," he repeated as he ran off toward his class.

Charlie and I headed for the kindergarten ceremony where he donned a blue cap with a striped tassel. He shook the teacher's hand and smiled a Cheshire cat grin for the picture. After he gobbled as many cookies and drank as much punch as I would allow, he ran outside to play with his buddies while I confirmed party plans with Austin's mother.

At 11:30 A.M., I dropped Charlie and Austin off at the karate studio. The gusty wind had died down, and it looked like rain was a given. *So much for the balloon fight,* I thought. *Oh well, they'll still have fun.* Alex and his friends Ellis and Cole would get to the party soon, since school had just let out.

I decided to get in a little shopping while the kids were busy and began driving toward a neighboring city. I got about half a mile down the road when my cell phone rang.

My husband was calling from his work in Greeley. "Honey, there is a bad storm coming toward Windsor. They're talking tornado."

"Do you think I should get the kids?" I asked. I wondered if the warning was just a false alarm.

"Yes!" he said, surprising me with his urgency. He was not the type to overreact. "You have about twenty minutes."

It takes ten to get home, I thought. *I can make it.* I made a hasty U-turn as hail began to ding my van. The dings turned into thumps, as the hail grew larger. My imagination pictured what might happen to the metal karate building if it were hit by a tornado. I knew I had to get them out of there.

Alex and his friends were dodging puddles and hail, running across the karate school parking lot when I drove up. I caught up to them inside after they had dropped all their school stuff and begun to play. "Boys," I said. "Get your things and get in the van. We need to go home, and we can come back in a little bit." They began to protest, but I stopped them short, "This is a bad storm, and we'll be safer at home." I quietly told the karate instructor about the impending tornado. "I'm taking these five boys to my basement," I said.

One of my son's friends overheard our conversation and began to panic. I clutched his shoulders and stared into his eyes. "It won't do us any good for you to get worried and panic," I said. "We need to do what we can to be safe. I need you to get in the van now, so we can go to my basement." He calmed down immediately, and we all piled into the van. I snapped the van transmission into gear and sped toward safety.

When I turned west, I saw the tornado. A black cloud lay low across the horizon to the southeast. I could see one short, wide pillar drop to the ground. It looked like a bad rainstorm and nothing like the funnel clouds you see in pictures or movies. The hail had grown from golf-ball-sized to baseball-sized and began making deafening thwacks against my windshield. I cringed with each hit, amazed that my windshield had not cracked. I paused at a red light, and then sped through, watching over my shoulder for the approaching tornado.

Then Alex's friend Cole said, "I think we should pray, Mrs. Cox."

"Good idea, Cole. Will you start us off?" I replied.

The nine-year-old boy prayed out loud for protection and safety. I prayed aloud after him. Then all six of us prayed silently together as the tornado approached. Drivers were stopping underneath trees for protection from the hail. So few people seemed to know a tornado was coming. I couldn't stop and warn them. I had five boys to get to safety.

I continued to pray. "Lord, please help us make it home safely. Please keep this windshield intact until we get home. Please protect us. Be here with us."

Suddenly, an ice ball thwacked the window, leaving multiple cracks. I drove on, praying that the windshield would hold until I got to my garage. I lost sight of the tornado when I turned north. I looked for it again when I turned west, but trees and houses blocked my view. I pushed the garage door opener again and again as I sped up to my driveway, but nothing happened. The power was out. I parked in the driveway and we ran to the front porch and then down into the basement. The hail was so loud we couldn't hear anything else.

I gathered candles, a lighter, batteries, a radio, and a headlamp. I tried to find the news on several radio stations, but nobody was talking about a tornado. The radio stations were playing music. A surreal feeling settled in my gut. Then the hail stopped.

I tried to call my husband. All circuits were busy. My oldest son, Christian, was still at his school. When could I leave and get to him? Was he safe? I tried to call the other mothers. I wanted them to know their kids were at my house. The circuits were still busy. Then my phone rang. It was Ellis' mom on my caller ID, but the signal faded before I answered.

I finally got through to my husband. He told me that the tornado had already passed through Windsor. That was all he knew. Eventually, I was able to call out and reassure the other kids' moms. Then, the boys and I headed out for Christian's school. I didn't know if he would be okay or what to expect when I got there. When I drove up, I saw that the building was intact. Tears caught in my throat and pooled in my eyes. We were all okay. We were safe. God had answered Cole's prayers for protection and our prayers for safety. I checked Christian out of school, and we drove home. The rest of the day was a scramble of phone calls to check on church members and friends.

It wasn't until I went to the devastated area the next day that I realized how close we had come to the tornado. We had been right in the path of the tornado just minutes before it swept through. It caused its greatest devastation just two blocks from the boys' school and karate studio. Entire buildings had been demolished; many second-stories were gone. Thankfully, the kids at the school and karate studio were unharmed. God had heard the prayers of five boys and me. He was there with us through the storm.

—*Nancy Osterholm Cox*

Two-Dollar
Treasure

*So let us come boldly to the throne of our gracious
God. There we will receive His mercy and we
will find grace to help us when we need it most.*

Hebrews 4:16

My children knew the Saturday morning routine. Pack snacks and sippy cups, then buckle in car seats for a morning of garage sales. We waved to our seminary neighbors, already leaving the starting gate on this beautiful summer morning.

"Mommy, who can get out at the first sale?" Alex asked. Our family tradition allowed for the children to take turns getting out at each yard sale.

"Let's see what they have, sweetheart. If they have books, you may have the first turn."

We rounded the corner into one of my favorite sale neighborhoods. When we saw the median littered with multiple signs, Jordan squealed. Even at two years old, he knew a top-notch garage sale neighborhood when he saw it.

My daughter, Rachel, wailed. "Mommy, there's something yucky in my cup."

I pulled up to the curb for our initial stop and leaned back to grasp the cup flailing through the air. It was the small things that made Rachel cry. Building blocks that would not obey her. Doll clothes that refused to fit her baby doll. Once, she threw a fit over a word she could not say just right.

I unscrewed the plastic lid, peered into the cup and found the culprit—a small piece of greenish plastic from my worn out dishwasher. Each day, when I opened the steaming dishwasher, I found small bits of green plastic and bits of rust sprinkled throughout my clean dishes. The bottom rack was disintegrating. My 1970's model Whirlpool had seen better days. Hard water and multiple renters had taken its toll.

With four small children and one on the way, I could not visualize myself washing our daily mountain of tableware by hand. I had two options. Take the bottom rack out and use only the top one washing dishes twice as often, or find a new rack for an extinct dishwasher. Neither alternative seemed realistic at this point in my morning. I fished out the plastic and returned the cup to my tearful toddler before inviting my oldest to join me on the driveway of our first conquest.

Shoes and toys lined both sides of the cement drive. Alex and I weaved through the tables and boxes searching for small treasures among tubes of half-used hand cream, cracked Tupperware lids, unmatched socks, and broken dishes. We often found worthwhile merchandise amid the junk. Why pay twenty dollars for a name brand when you can get the same thing for fifty cents? Many seminary families like ours relied on God-given opportunities like weekend rummage sales in lieu of a trip to the mall.

I heard a shout from the van window where little faces peered out in anticipation. "Bike, Mommy!" I smiled and waved, knowing I only had seven dollars to spend. A bike was not in the budget, unless it was free. We passed by many great items. Alex beamed with excitement as we returned to the van with her ten-cent book in hand. Then, we loaded up for the short trip down the street to find another sale.

The sales were typical. We found children's shoes for fifty cents and a small bookshelf for a dollar. Driveways strewn with fishing gear or grandmother's knick-knacks received a "thumbs down" from my crew. Soon little heads drooped from the lull of the car engine. A small sigh left my lips. With a couple of dollars left, I pondered in the precious silence.

What did I really need? The kids had enough toys and clothes. Our house was adequately stocked with furniture and books. We had a working toaster and even a bread machine. My mind wandered to the dishwasher. Checking to be sure the kids were asleep in the back, I looked upward and spoke boldly. "Lord, what I really need is the bottom rack to a dishwasher."

Meandering through the neighborhood, I realized it was almost noon. The last three yards were sparsely littered with leftovers, and the garage sale fanatics had gone home for lunch. I had resolved to turn south and head back to the seminary campus we called home when a small sign caught my eye. Instinctively, I turned the van down the next street. "One quick look can't hurt," I said.

As I approached the small sale, my heart quickened. What was that on the driveway? My feet were out the door before the van stopped rolling. Right in front of me was a mint condition, avocado green, bottom rack to a dishwasher. Thoughts swirled through my head as I stared in amazement. Was this some kind of a joke? Could this be real?

I barely noticed when a middle-aged woman approached me. "You know," she said, "I was going to throw this away, but this morning I felt like God was telling me to put it out because someone needed it. It's two dollars. Do you want it?"

I nodded my head and told her the story as she tucked the bills into her little pouch. Then with a friendly hug she sent me on my way. Filled with awe, I pulled away from the curb and turned toward home. There was no doubt in my mind that the real treasure I discovered that day was far more important than a dish rack.

—Casey Pitts

Shedding the Cloak of Fear

*Honor your father and mother. Then
you will live a long, full life in the land
the Lord your God is giving you.*

Genesis 20:12

On a cloudy Memorial Day, we packed the kids in the car, bought some geraniums, and made the pilgrimage to my father's grave. It had been a tenuous journey to reconnect with my father after so many years of alienation. As a paranoid schizophrenic, he lived a solitary life after my parents divorced when I was five. During the late 1950s, it was illegal to divorce someone who was mentally ill, but because my father was abusive, the court allowed my mother to divorce him.

To protect us, my uncles arrived one morning to move our belongings to an undisclosed rental house. We had to be vigilant while we played in the front yard in case my father drove by in the Jeep he used to make deliveries for his dry cleaning business. When the green Jeep appeared, we would dart into the house, lest he discover where we lived. I was afraid he would kidnap us. Later, when my mother purchased a home, he found out where we lived. I recall peeking out my bedroom window every Saturday morning while he revved the engine of his green Jeep in front of our house, hoping to catch a glimpse of us.

For forty years, I lived in fear. I harbored a great deal of anger after being deprived of a loving relationship with my dad. I struggled greatly with the fifth commandment, Exodus 20:12: "Honor your father and your mother, so that you may live long in the land the Lord your God is giving you." It's the only commandment that gives an instruction and a promise that comes with fulfilling it. I wondered how I could ever honor my own father, the source of so much pain in my life. Five years ago, the Lord brought this verse to mind repeatedly, and during my prayer time, I felt His encouragement for me to make contact with my dad.

Full of trepidation, I invited him to our home for lunch. My brother and I picked him up at the bus station. Unlike the gargoyle image my fear had created, my dad was a dapper gentleman, fastidiously dressed with a sport coat and hat. Decked out like a refined eastern prep school gentleman caught in a fashion time warp of the 1940s, he arrived with a gift for everyone.

Apparently, age had softened his emotional difficulties. At eighty, he had a childlike charm and graciousness. He chuckled quietly as his young grandchildren chattered away and was delighted with my son's challenge to a game of chess. In his younger days, my father was a chess master. He was very proud of his Anglican priest son-in-law and couldn't bring himself to call my husband anything but Reverend Cobb.

Gradually, I became aware of the heavy, suffocating cloak of anxiety and alienation I had worn for forty years. My brother told me a story my dad had related to him. When I was in high school, I rode on a float in a Fourth of July parade. My father was standing on the parade route in front of his business. Apparently, he thought I looked at him and turned my head away. Since we didn't communicate in the years that followed, he felt I had rejected him and was very sad about that. It must have been heartbreaking to live with that perceived rejection for most of his life, and I began to imagine what our reconnection meant to him.

When my father died a few years later, it fell to me to deal with his personal effects. It was peculiar sorting through his belongings, catching only glimpses of his complicated life. As I went through his files, a yellowed piece of paper floated out of a file onto the floor. I was about to throw it away, but upon inspection, I realized it revealed the mystery of the location of the cemetery where my grandmother was buried. After making inquiries, I learned we had a family grave plot filled with eastern relations in Watertown, Massachusetts. We resolved to bury my father there.

We wanted to do a graveside service with my children. The large marker for the family plot looked Anglican, even though my father's family were Methodists. Its curved shape reminded me of the stained glass windows, which lined the sides of our church. Remarkably, the beautiful Canterbury cross at the center of the marker looked similar to the cross my husband and I had engraved on our wedding rings. I was comforted by the existence and style of the cross.

It was but a thread in the fabric of generations of faith being transmitted from parent to child in our family. Somehow, the daily struggle of modeling the faith for my children was lightened by the reassurance of God's merciful design for our family. Were great-grandmother Clara's prayers fulfilled as her great-grandchildren planted flowers at her headstone to honor her life these many years later? With the service, I felt a sense of acceptance and closure around the memories of my dad.

The disturbing early experiences with my father are still part of my life, but they no longer have a stifling grip on me. The apprehension, anger, and alienation have been replaced with a mature understanding of a man who "knows not what he did," and the blessing that occurred when my crippling fear was replaced with a delightful memory. Through my father's death, I met my half-brother, Jimmy, who is a devout Christian and possesses the same charm and humility I encountered in my dad. It was another blessing that came from being obedient to the fifth commandment.

I am grateful my conscience is clear before God. I honored my father, not because he deserved it, but because of what Christ did for me. As a result, I can claim the promise of a long, full life for my family and me in the land the Lord has given us.

—*Holly Packard Cobb*

Andy the Handyman

If we confess our sins to him, he is faith-
ful and just to forgive us our sins and
to cleanse us from all wickedness.

1 John 1:9

"Which drain is it?" Dad asked as he stood at my front door with a flashlight in one hand and a toolbox in the other.

Dad has graced my doorstep more times than I can count, clothed in denim overalls with a box of tools at his side. I still remember the old red box he carried long ago. I was too tiny to lift it, but I was plenty big enough to pass him each tool. The words "Andy the Handyman" were handwritten in permanent marker across the top. I don't know if Dad wrote it himself, or if it was the work of a pen-happy child, but the label fit him well.

I recall watching Dad replace the pickets in our fence. I traced each letter with my finger, while the heat of the sun warmed my hand. The notes of his whistle moved through air, like seeds carried away in the breeze. A few of those seeds took root in my heart, where they bloomed over time in the garden of love for my dad.

When we needed our roof repaired, Dad climbed the ladder to fix the shingles. When we moved, he was there to pack the truck, and when we built a family room, he helped lay sheets of drywall. I had grown so accustomed to picking up the phone to ask for his help, that when we encountered a little plumbing problem, I didn't hesitate to give him a call.

My husband and I have been plagued with drainage problems in every single bathtub in every single house we've owned. When we finally moved into a new house with a shiny white tub and new fixtures, we assumed those days were behind us, but within two months we were dealing with a disinclined drain tub once more. A few trips to the grocery store for "Dr. Plummer" seemed affordable enough, but after the fourth trip, we felt like we were putting the doctor through college.

I was getting more than a little cranky wading through a ditch of stagnant water every morning. Perhaps Michael was washing fishing wire down the drain. Maybe it was bacon grease or buckets of drywall compound—who knows what men do? Since I couldn't figure out how to remove the stopper, let alone discover the culprit, I sent Dad upstairs with the hope that my "Jack of all trades" could rehabilitate our temperamental tub.

Dad focused a strong light on the drain and lowered his screwdriver into the darkness. I held my breath and waited for him to find Michael's sock, his tie, or maybe even his Levis. With a few turns of his wrist, Dad released the plug. Daylight streamed through the window, into the drain, exposing the undeniable evidence of a fifteen-year-old dispute. A wad of blonde hair with a suspicious resemblance to my own, lay nestled in the drain.

Without hesitation, Dad pulled at the hair with his hands, releasing each tangled strand, and then passed it my way. "Any more?" he asked. His tone suggested he was ready to take on another tub or two—maybe three.

"No, this is the only one we've been having trouble with," I replied, staring at the wet wig in my hands.

After Dad left, I couldn't stop thinking about the monstrosity he yanked from the drain. Then I realized why our family of seven females had never suffered from slow drain syndrome when I was growing up. Dad had taken care of the problem before it got out of hand, but since I moved in with Michael, the hair just kept collecting in the drain until the water rose to our shins.

In many ways, the relationship with my dad mirrors the one between my Heavenly Father and me. God is always knocking on my door, ready with His toolbox to fix my problems. All He needs from me is an invitation to come in with His light to show me the way and His promise to cleanse me from sin.

Throughout my whole life, God has been looking after the many things I've taken for granted. The hidden sins of my life have been there, even when I haven't been aware of them. As my faith has matured, God's light has made it possible for me to see my mistakes more clearly. I now realize that His mercy prevents them from accumulating, and His forgiveness continues to provide me with a clean slate. Like seeds on the wind, God's promises have taken hold in my heart, where they have since bloomed over time, in the garden of love for my Heavenly Father. I know I can safely stand on His Word without doubt, and I know He'll be there each time I call.

—*Darlene Schacht*

A Forever Family

For the Lord is good.
His unfailing love continues forever,
and his faithfulness continues to each generation.

                                        Psalm 100:5

I t was a typical maternity ward, filled with frantic doctors and nurses rushing about, but hospital personnel had thoughtfully provided a private room for our family. Our daughter had insisted on a dedication ceremony and an opportunity to say goodbye. She planned the ceremony; our job was to gather together. My husband positioned himself beside me with our daughter in her wheelchair next to her father. Our pastor stood with his arm on the back of her chair, and the adoptive family and their two-year-old daughter completed the circle.

Grandpa picked up his tiny granddaughter with trembling arms. Tears ran freely down his face as he prayed for her future. When he placed the infant in my arms, my chin quivered. We knew this moment was inevitable, but my tears fell, wetting the blanket wrapped around my grandchild. I prayed and gave her to her mother. She held the baby to her chest, and everybody cried. She sang a song and lifted the baby to our pastor.

As he prayed, he trickled tiny specks of oil on her little forehead. I couldn't help but wonder what my daughter's future held. Her tears made it difficult to hope she would ever be happy again. When the adoptive mother cradled our grandchild in her arms, her husband looked across the room and smiled at my daughter as if to say, "You've done a courageous thing."

At the end of the ceremony, our precious grandchild was returned to the maternity ward. As my husband pushed our daughter back to her room, she turned and looked up at him. "I can't believe I just gave my baby away."

"I know honey," he replied. "Stay close to me. We'll get through this, somehow."

It may sound trite, but time truly does bring healing. Years later, we found ourselves in another hospital, pressed up against the door to another delivery room.

"I think I hear his cry." I said. As I leaned closer, I heard a clear, turbulent newborn cry. Overcome with joy, I turned to my husband. He couldn't hear, so I was doing the listening for him. "Michael's here, honey," I whispered.

"What did you say?"

"Michael just greeted the world!" We hugged each other as people walked down the hallway. They didn't know a miracle had occurred. They didn't know a hole in our hearts had been filled.

One year later, we traveled to see our little grandson. Mikie was prepared to take his first step, and we were standing by to capture the moment. With my camera poised and ready, I watched my husband sit on the floor and beckon to Michael. I was overcome with happiness, as I listened to my husband.

"Come on, Mikie. It's okay. I'll catch you if you fall. You can do it!" Michael toddled over to his grandpa.

Tears filled my eyes as I remembered another occasion. Our daughter was leaving the hospital after placing her child in another mother's arms. As she stood up from her wheelchair, her daddy said, "Come on, honey. I'll catch you if you stumble."

One year later, we moved out of state to live closer to Michael. He was now in preschool, while his mommy worked full-time to help her family. Life was busy. When Michael was almost three years old, a miracle occurred. One morning, as my daughter left for work, she pulled out the day's mail from the mailbox and threw it on the seat of her car. A fat yellow envelope caught her eye, and she ripped it open.

A letter and pictures tumbled out. Grabbing the letter, she began to read.

"Dear Mom,

I want to come and see you. My parents say it's okay, as I just turned eighteen. We all want to come: Dad, Mom, Grandpa, Grandma, and my sister. Please let me know when the best time would be. I want to meet you!"

Love, Rebecca."

Rebecca's family arrived and assembled at our house for a grand reunion. Our prayers had been answered. Rebecca had grown into a beautiful, young woman. It was remarkable how she loved to do the same things as her birth mother. It was a time of singing, sharing, and crying. As I sat on the couch, listening to their conversations, I felt so blessed.

"Oh, look at that picture. I love to ride horses, too."

"And our hair color is identical."

Their words brought a smile to my face. It was absolutely beautiful how God had transformed our sorrow into joy. Hope had been reborn. My husband smiled at me, and we clasped hands.

Months later, we had another reunion. We took Rebecca and Mikie to meet our extended family. As we drove along, we sang, talked, and watched the scenery roll by. Sister and brother were riding in the back seat when, suddenly, they began to giggle.

"You're a monkey," she said.

"No, you're a monkey," he replied. Laughter erupted and filled the car. What a beautiful sound!

When I turned to look at my husband, I saw his tears. *Isn't God wonderful?* I thought. He not only touched our daughter's heart and gave her hope, but also he touched a couple of grandparent's hearts in the process. It was truly amazing to hear our grandchildren laughing together.

All the uncles, aunts and cousins greeted their new relative. She shared the same creative talents as the family, and they accepted her with hugs and warmth. After a few days, it started to snow, so we returned to her house. We were faced with another goodbye, and I knew Mikie was saddened.

When our big, old Silverado truck pulled into her driveway, we snapped off our seatbelts, and jumped out of the truck. Then, we ran as fast as we could to the front yard to make snow angels. Later, when I thought about that day, I believe that we all had the same idea.

"Let's leave an imprint in the snow," I said. "Something to remember." So, I grabbed Mikie, and the three of us plopped down in the snow and made angels.

Later, we all stood for a moment on the front steps of her house—a home we'd never dreamed of visiting. My husband wrapped his arms around Mikie and gathered us together. He looked at his family and put his arms around us. "Come on guys," he said. "It's okay. This time, we are not saying goodbye. Our family is a forever thing, you know."

"Like making angels in the snow," Rebecca said.

—*Shirley A. Reynolds*

Answer
Your Door

Look! I stand at the door and knock. If
you hear my voice and open the door, I will
come in, and we will share a meal together
as friends. Those who are victorious will sit
with me on my throne, just as I was victori-
ous and sat with my Father on his throne.

Revelation 3:20–21

At what point, exactly, did my life start falling apart?
I wondered as I sat silently, vacantly staring out
the window at my children as they rode their scoot-
ers up and down the sidewalk. That's just the thing.
There wasn't one particular incident or time that
became a turning point, hurling my life into a fast,
downward spiral. But isn't that how it normally goes?
Somewhere along the way, we buy into a lie. Then we

get caught in a web of deceit that chips away at our faith little by little. Finally, one morning we find ourselves immersed in depression and hopelessness. Now, here I was, spending my days staring out windows, not caring what the next day would bring.

I had drifted so far from the point at which my husband, Derrick, and I were first married. We were committed Christians who deeply loved the Lord and spent much time in prayer, in His word, and serving others. Frankly, there wasn't much time to worry about myself. I think that's how the Lord intends it. Serve Him with all our heart, and keep our mind off ourselves!

Somewhere along my journey with God, I traded the truth for a lie. A desire to escape from my routine and "normal" life led me in search of something—anything—to fill the perceived vacuum inside. For some reason, I wanted more.

Derrick started making a lot of money at his director-level position in a high-technology field, and between our two incomes, the "more" that I wanted was easily attainable. He would come home from work with announcements of, "Let's go to the mountains this weekend!" Or, "Let's spend a week at a bed and breakfast!" Soon, our days and nights were consumed with entertainment, travel, and toys.

This was wonderful—until we started having children, and then, there just wasn't time to get away. From the onset of motherhood, I poured my entire life and being into my kids. Since I couldn't do all that I wanted anymore, I tried to satisfy my restlessness through my children. We were always on the go, searching for entertainment, or shopping for the latest and greatest toys.

Even with three young children to keep me busy, I still kept searching for the missing piece to my life's puzzle. I decided to start a home-based business to have something I could call my own. *Surely, this will fill the void inside,* I told myself. Instead, it made me crazy. I found myself yelling at my children for the smallest things, becoming distant to my husband, and breaking down in tears because I couldn't keep up with the laundry. *Other mothers can handle this, why can't I?* I'd ask myself time and time again. I felt like a failure as a mom, as a wife, and even as a Christian. I couldn't understand where I'd gone wrong. I still loved the Lord, went to church, and was involved in many church activities. Granted, I didn't have a lot of time to pray anymore, but with three kids, a household to run, church commitments to maintain, and a home-based business to get off the ground, I figured God understood if I had to pray "on the fly" during this season.

I did my best to maintain my supermom image, continually trying to balance my entire life on a single thread. Then one day, it all came crashing down. I had finally reached the end. No hope, no peace, no way out. In complete and utter desperation, I threw myself across my bed and cried out, "God, why aren't You helping me? I cannot take anymore. Not even one more day!"

Somehow, God's whisper made it past the tears and past the torment, and I heard His voice in my heart. "I can't." That couldn't be God speaking, could it? After all, He's God! He can do anything. What does He mean, "I can't"? I could now add confusion to the array of emotions I was experiencing at that moment. I heard nothing more.

I prayed and sought God with all my might over the next few days. The still small voice did not return. Just when I was about to chalk it up to my own mind speaking to me, God confirmed His words to me during the following Sunday morning church service.

"God's not pushy," my pastor declared. "He's not going to force His will on you. The choice is always yours." And then he spoke the words—God's words—that changed my entire world in one moment. "In Revelation 3:20, Jesus offers us an amazing invitation," the pastor said as he continued. "He says, 'I stand at the door and knock. If you hear my voice and open the door, I will come in, and we will share a meal together as friends.' Jesus so badly wants to be your friend," my pastor said, "but we first have to open the door and let Him in."

His words were like a golden ray of sunlight slicing through a stormy sky. Now, I understood that God *was* trying to help me, but I wasn't letting Him. How many times had He gently rapped on the door of my heart, but I refused to open it? If I had answered the door, I would have found all the peace, rest, and sanity I was searching for. I began to remember the many times I had left Jesus standing on my porch.

The times I came home from a long day at work and turned on the television so I didn't have to think, and Jesus came knocking. *Come sit with me instead. I'll refresh you.*

Then, there were the times when Derrick and I finally had some time to ourselves without the kids, and we chose to run off and be entertained. Jesus again came knocking. *When two or three are gathered together, I am in your midst. Pray together for your marriage. I will strengthen it.* How about the times I got so busy working that I tried to rush the kids out of the house to play, and Jesus once again came knocking. *Sit and read My Word to them. I will draw you close as a family.*

The tears began flowing again—right there in church—but this time, they weren't tears of depression or discouragement. They were tears of hope. I saw how I had fallen off the path of life and how much God must love me to continually try to woo me back. My eyes were opened to how I was kept busy "chasing my own tail," searching for something I already possessed—true fulfillment in Jesus Christ.

I recommitted myself to God that instant. "Lord, give me a sensitive heart toward You. Help me clearly hear your voice and be quick to obey. I don't ever want to ignore You when You knock on my door again."

Since that moment of rededication, I have returned to diligently seeking the Lord. I am busier than ever, but God now gets the best part of my day, every day. I realize that if I desire a strong relationship with God and want to enjoy the peace that flows from that relationship, it's up to me to cultivate it. James 4:8 tells us that when we come close to God, He will come close to us. We have to take the first step. If we don't move toward God, we will move away from Him. There is no neutral gear.

Don't ever buy the lie that God is not present in your circumstances or does not care about you. His still small voice is always beckoning you to come and get away with Him. Be sure to answer the door. Because there is no one, no thing, or no place that will satisfy you as He does.

—*Renee Gray-Wilburn*

Instant
Traditions

God places the lonely in families;
He sets the prisoners free and gives them joy.

Psalm 68:6

I stood by the front door, joking with the other teens and their parents as they struggled into heavy coats and scarves against the November snow. As each family left, my spirits rose. With a last, "Best pecan pie you've ever made," Mother closed the door behind the last visitor. As soon as I heard the click of the latch, I disappeared up the stairs, down the hall, into the frigid attic.

Two minutes later, I was back, balancing a stack of dusty boxes. I set them on the coffee table in the living room and paused for a moment: should I go for more, or start with what I had? I made my decision, moving the magazines and ashtrays from the end table and pulling a frayed, green mat from the top box. This was the grass; the stable went on it, pushed against the lamp base. I smiled at the pipe-playing shepherd boy in my hands. Where did I want Amahl to stand this year?

I heard my father's uneven step and looked around. He was moving the card table away from the front window to make room for the Christmas tree. After all, Thanksgiving had officially ended when the last guest left, and now, it was time for Christmas decorating. Daddy turned on the Christmas records he had organized that morning. Within minutes, I could hear Mother in the kitchen, singing along.

That was how we'd always done it, so that's how we always did it. We laughingly called it "instant tradition." The presents were always on the piano, thanks to the years of owning a dog who chewed anything under the tree. The tip of the tree was wired to the wall because, one year, Granny almost pulled it over as she adjusted an ornament. The menu for Christmas dinner, the plans for Christmas Eve, even the playing order of the caroling records—our family did it our way.

We applied the instant tradition principle to all holidays, but Christmas was the best. All of our family quirks and memories were at their most potent during that month long season. There were only the three of us, plus Granny and the dog, of course, but we could easily spend four hours opening gifts on Christmas morning. First, everything was handed out, and the piles counted. Then we figured out the rotation so that we'd come out even at the end. Presents were opened in a strict order, building to the most exciting one, and the recipient had to fully admire each gift before the next person's turn.

Nothing changed when I grew up. Some of the timing had to be tweaked because I had a husband and job 800 miles from home, but that didn't matter. Our family wasn't about to miss a tradition.

"My class was completely out of control today," I said with a laugh as we left the airport.

"Since your plane came in so late," Daddy said, "we thought we'd better get the tree on our way home."

"My family finally decided an artificial tree was simpler," my husband said, but we ignored this travesty. Our Christmas tree was always a Douglas fir, seven-and-a-half feet high, no bare spots, and one flat side for the window. How could anyone consider anything but a fresh tree?

My husband waited as we checked every Douglas fir at the tree lot and then carefully centered it in the window at home. He tried to help with the strings of lights, but he could never get it quite right and usually ended up watching the rest of us with a bemused expression on his face. The last decorations, even after the tinsel, were the family egg-ornaments—one for each of us. Mother had found another one somewhere and painted my husband's name on it, and I coached him in the proper hanging technique.

"Best tree we've ever had!" Mother said, as we admired the lights reflected in the ornaments.

"At this rate, we're approaching perfection!"

I grinned at my sleepy spouse. Someone said that every year. After all, it was part of the tradition.

Even tradition can't stop the relentless march of time. Granny died, missing her 100th birthday by only a few years. My marriage ended in divorce, but I continued to fly home for Christmas. When Mother died after thirty-eight years of multiple sclerosis, Daddy and I clung to all the traditions, reminiscing over a Christmas dinner of Rock Cornish game hen with wild rice. Two years later, my father passed away, and I no longer had any reason to go home for the holidays.

I began attending a new church, after three decades at my previous one. And suddenly, it was almost Christmas again—with no traditions in place. "It probably sounds silly," I admitted to my friends, "but I still want to have my stocking on Christmas morning, even if I have to fill it myself. I want to go caroling, and write silly tags for presents. I know we had our flaws, but Christmas is a time for families."

"You're right," Ruth replied and smiled. "God created families, starting with Adam and Eve, so they must be important to Him."

"We want you to come for Thanksgiving dinner," Traci said. "Ruth and her family will be there, too."

Thanksgiving afternoon I looked at my forkful of hot turkey. There was a small Christmas tree in the center of the table, and ornaments on the stair railing. I opened my mouth to say, "Well, *we* always . . ." and stopped. *Different family, different traditions*, I told myself firmly.

Traci asked about my plans for Christmas. "I'm not sure yet," I said tentatively. "We'll just see, I guess. Thanks so much for including me today!"

I walked into Sunday school a couple of weeks before Christmas and found a seat near the wall. A woman named Lynn walked over and sat next to me. "How are you doing today?" she asked.

"It can get a little lonely this time of year," I admitted.

"Oh, I know!" she replied. "I'll be seeing my son and his family after Christmas, but I'm spending the day itself with friends. Do you have plans?"

"Actually, by God's grace, I do," I said.

After the service, I met Ruth in the aisle. "I want to celebrate Christmas with you before we leave for the holiday," she said. "Are you free for lunch next Saturday?"

"That's dress rehearsal for the choir program," I replied.

"How about Monday?"

"Plans with friends."

"Tuesday?"

"Christmas party with the Bible study ladies."

Ruth laughed. "You're a popular woman," she said, and we finally settled on Wednesday.

Christmas morning found me at another friend's house. The gifts were under the tree, and my stocking was leaning against the windowsill. *Different family, different traditions*, I reminded myself once again. And after all, what did it matter? The most important tradition was to celebrate the birth of Jesus Christ. And I had been doing that very thing in abundance—with my new "family."

—*Elsi Dodge*

Heavenly
Higher Math

*And everyone who has given up houses or broth-
ers or sisters or father or mother or children or
property, for my sake, will receive a hundred times
as much in return and will inherit eternal life.*

Matthew 19:29

Did you have a subject in school you tried to avoid? Mine was math. I still remember sitting in my geometry class and wondering if my teacher was speaking English. A few words sounded familiar, but I couldn't put them into any kind of context. I looked around to see if this unknown language confused any other students, but I found no support; I appeared to be the only one in the dark. It was then I forged a plan to elude math as much as possible. My strategy followed me to college where I pursued a degree in psychology and escaped courses like algebra. While I thought this was a surefire plan of avoidance, the Lord decided otherwise and enrolled me in His math course in the school of faith.

I registered for this divine education when I received His free gift of salvation and gave Him authority over my life. Consequently, God asked me kindly to give Him things and place my trust in His care. These things were minor at first. He asked me to give Him my time for church on Sunday mornings and for Bible study on Wednesday evenings. Then He asked me for some one-on-one time with Him each day. With every exchange, my confidence in His great care grew. I learned that when He subtracted something from me, it wasn't a loss but a gain. He added peace, protection, and value to my turbulent life. The more I gave, the more I gained.

My schooling in God's math continued over the next few years. He asked me to give Him my vocational aspirations, my future life-partner plans, and my dreams for the life I thought I needed. With every subtraction, I received an addition of peace and intimacy with Him. The subtractions became less difficult to make, and I began thinking I had finally graduated from His remedial math course.

Then the big test came. It took me by surprise because I thought the matter had already been settled, but the Lord knew better. He sent me to a real-life math class where I found myself sitting with folded arms and a hardened heart. Before the class, I even muttered to my husband, "We don't need this. It's ridiculous that we are being required to take this course." Our senior pastor intended to offer a financial program to the church, but first, he wanted the ministerial staff to participate and implement the practices found in the course. So, I attended— kicking and screaming.

The program consisted of Biblical lessons on the principles of stewardship. Once the lessons were completed, each family met with a counselor who looked over their finances and worked with them to establish a budget. I decided it was getting too personal. I handled our household budget, and we were doing just fine. Three minutes into the meeting, my delusions were quickly shattered. We left the counseling session with challenge to live for the next two months by the budget we had just created and to use cash for specific purchases. After a two-month trial period, we would meet with the counselor again to re-evaluate and readjust as needed.

My head was pounding as we walked out, and I was still grumbling about the foolishness of the whole project. For the sake of my husband's job, I resolved to give it a try for the trial period. The next two months were tough. We had to cut back on eating out, and the little treats in the grocery line never made it into the cart. Despite this, I remained determined to give the program a chance.

As my obedience grew, my obstinacy diminished. Toward the end of the trial period, my eyes began opening to the many blessings the Lord was pouring out. They were subtle blessings, easily overlooked by the casual eye, but God allowed me to see them. One such blessing came as my family and I were returning home from a visit with friends. Three deer leapt from the side of the road and crossed the highway just seconds away from a collision with our vehicle. After the initial shock, I knew the Lord had protected us from harm and prevented our car from being totaled. Good fortune? Not even close.

Another blessing occurred during a meal out with our allotted "entertainment" cash. When my husband went to pay for our dinner, the cashier told him that someone had already taken care of our bill. I began recording the blessings and quickly filled a number of pages in my journal. With each entry, the Lord continued to prove His promise from Matthew 19:29.

When we met with the counselor, I was ready to give God control of the finances He had entrusted to my care. My husband and I also entered a covenant with the Lord to live by a budget. We would not go into debt for anything but a house or a small business. As we left the meeting, I knew the Lord had subtracted the control of our finances from us, but instead of feeling powerless and empty, I felt relieved and secure.

A few months after our decision, I hit a snag. My three-year-old son had outgrown his shoes and needed another pair. Our clothing account was tight, and I only had a small amount of money. When we entered the shoe store, something caught Parker's eye. He went straight to the back, grabbed a pair of shoes off the shelf and quickly put them on. He stood and proudly displayed a pair of multicolored galoshes. "I want these ones, Mommy!" he said.

For the next few minutes, he followed me around the store listing the reasons why he needed the boots. My heart was breaking as I began to rationalize. *Could I borrow from Peter to pay Paul? It wouldn't hurt just this once.* Still, I knew I had given the Lord control, and I couldn't take it back. So, I left the store with a pair of practical tennis shoes and a very unhappy three-year-old.

The days went by, and I had forgotten about the incident when there was a knock at the door. I opened it to find a giant box at our doorstop, and I recognized the return address as my husband's cousin from the West Coast whom I had met only once. With Parker as an eager assistant, I lugged the box into the living room and cut it open. He pulled out clothes, a car seat, a backpack, books, puzzles, toys, and more. I choked back the tears. "Oh, Parker," I said, "Jesus has given us these wonderful things through Dad's cousin. It's a blessing box from the Lord."

The box was almost empty when Parker reached in one last time. He stood up and turned to me with a huge grin. "Look, Mom, Jesus gave me my galoshes." In his hands, he held a pair of bright yellow galoshes decorated with dinosaurs. I wept a little and laughed a lot as I watched my little guy slip on his new boots. "Galoshes," I whispered in a voice full of awe. "You even remembered Parker's galoshes. Thank You so much!"

Those yellow galoshes became a memorial to my family, and they have served as a reminder for us to trust the heart of God. He will never ask us to subtract anything from our lives without providing an abundance of His blessings. That's God's way. That's His higher math.

—*Kendis Chenoweth*

Hearing Voices Doesn't
Mean You're Crazy

For I am about to do something new.
See, I have already begun!

Isaiah 43:19

I had yet to open my eyes and greet the day when I
heard the voice. Not an audible voice, but something deep within my spirit distinctly speaking to
me. "Pray for your unborn son."

My eyes flew open immediately, and I looked
around. "Who was that? Is someone here?" I eyed
the closet thinking someone might jump out and
shout, "Surprise!" but no one did. I was alone. Well,
not exactly alone. God was there.

As a fairly new Christian, I wasn't accustomed
to the still, small voice God uses to impress truth
within our spirits. Because my day-to-day fellowship

with Him was still a bit unfamiliar, I assumed I'd been dreaming. Either that, or I was crazy. I laid in silence, hidden under a mound of blankets, and tried to make sense of what I thought I had heard.

Of all the things to hear at that time in my life, "Pray for your unborn son," made the least sense. Eight years before, I had lost my first son to sudden infant death syndrome. I was now raising two daughters, one of them determined to fulfill every requirement of the "terrible twos" down to the last tantrum. The last thing I wanted to think about was having more children, let alone praying for another son.

I tried my best to dismiss what I thought I had heard, but the five little words kept tugging at my heart. Finally, out of desperation to silence the nagging thoughts, I dropped to my knees and prayed. "God, I don't know if this is coming from you, but I think you're telling me to pray for my unborn son."

Over the next few weeks, the story in 1 Samuel of Hannah praying for a son was everywhere I turned. I heard it during sermons at church, as I listened to the radio, or when I talked to other Christians. It seemed obvious to me that God was going out of His way to let me know it was His voice that spoke to my heart that morning. Once I understood that He was calling me to pray and believe for my unborn son, I brought the great news to my husband, assuming he would be just as excited as I was. He wasn't.

At the time, he was working full-time and taking up to twelve units of college courses per semester. Although I was the primary care giver to our children, he too had been affected by our youngest daughter's behavior. The many demands he faced made it difficult for him to even consider having another child.

At that point, I believed I was following a direct command from God, and while I understood my husband's lack of excitement, his reaction was disheartening. Nevertheless, I began to pray for everything from my hidden fears of having a safe pregnancy and delivery to my unborn son's future ministry, job, friends, wife, and children. At any moment, my husband would realize I was right—or at least that's what I hoped. He would believe I had heard from God, and soon, he would heed God's voice and begin praying for his unborn son.

It took five long years until my husband opened his heart enough to consider the possibility. During those five years, I wavered between doubt and faith. I found myself growing weary of praying for something that might never come to pass. I longed to have someone with whom to share my prayers and my conviction in what I believed God was telling me.

The few people I took into my confidence thought my desires stemmed from the loss of my first son.

On more than one occasion I cried out to God, letting Him know in no uncertain terms that "He started this." There were moments when I felt so incredibly alone. During those times, I asked God to take the desire away if it wasn't truly from Him or if I had fabricated it as some people around me had implied.

I found myself identifying greatly with the woman in the Bible who helped the prophet Elijah. Elijah told her she would have a son. Instead of jumping up and down because her heart's desire would finally come to pass, her initial reaction was, "Please don't joke; I couldn't bear it." Honestly, when I felt I could no longer bear it, I would throw my own tantrum, acting worse than any two-year-old ever could. Thankfully, regardless of my behavior, God managed to find unique ways to confirm His original command. "Pray for your unborn son."

In the spring of 1999, after yet another, "don't-joke-I-couldn't-bear-it" session with God, I went to church. I set aside my concerns and began to enjoy the worship music. In the midst of worship, I heard that same soft, distinct voice speak to my heart. This time, it wasn't just the command to pray for my unborn son, it was followed by a promise, "Behold, I do a new thing." To my surprise, I didn't have to ask for a hundred confirmations or a specific revelation. A tremendous peace came over me, and I instantly knew what God was saying. Through the promise of Isaiah 43:19, God caused me to understand that in the year 2000, He would bring about new things, including my unborn son.

It didn't matter that it seemed impossible. God had given His Word. A few days later, as a step of faith, I painted a miniature wooden horse on a rocker and underneath the piece wrote, "To my son, I love you." I put the date on it so my son would know he had been the fulfillment of God's promise. Though I still wasn't pregnant, and my husband had not yet fully caught the vision, I wanted my child to know he had been prayed for long before his birth.

After painting the horse, I shared it with my husband and reminded him of God's words. Though he was not yet convinced that having another child was what he wanted, he began to acknowledge God might be leading our family in that direction. He came as close to agreement as he could by finally saying he "might be okay with it." One month later, I found out I was pregnant.

The most incredible part about this whole story was at the moment my pregnancy was confirmed, my husband took my hands in his to pray. And his very first words were, "Thank you, God, for our son."

By faith, all of my husband's doubts and concerns had fallen away, and he knew. On other the hand, I— the one who had believed and prayed for five years— began to worry. Faced with the reality of words spoken five years earlier, I was flooded with doubt and stress. What if I was wrong? What if something happened to this baby? What if it was a girl?

My uncertainty after years of praying and believing for my unborn son made me feel like a failure, but none of my feelings came as a surprise to God. He knew the struggles I would face when He asked me to pray for my unborn son. He knew my husband would initially reject the idea, He also knew I needed time to work through the fears I had from losing my first son in order to trust Him enough to give me another son. God knew the many questions that would torment me and still, He was faithful. While He allowed me to struggle through my misgivings, He made it abundantly clear He was by my side every step of the way.

On January 1, 2000, God's promise was fulfilled. I no longer had to pray for my unborn son as God brought him forth and received all the glory.

—Monica Cane

A Miraculous Push

*Then Jesus said to the disciples, "Have faith
in God. I tell you the truth, you can say
to this mountain, 'May you be lifted up
and thrown into the sea,' and it will happen. But you must really believe it will happen and have no doubt in your heart."*

Mark 11:22–24

We pushed and we shoved, but the big, old
thing wouldn't budge an inch. Obviously,
we were stranded in an isolated valley in a rugged
mountainous region of New South Wales, Australia,
and we knew we were in big trouble.

As leaders of the wilderness camp for a group of
young college students—many from broken homes—
we spent most nights talking about learning to trust

God, often in seemingly impossible situations. We were camped in a deserted farmhouse with a cheery fireplace where we gathered each evening. One night, our main text was from Mark 11:22–25, and the questions flew thick and fast. We used this and other passages to demonstrate that as long as we lived according to God's Will and acted in obedience to His Word, we could trust Him to fulfill His promises.

Each day, we left the house to explore the wilderness around us. We returned by nightfall, weary and hungry. After a hearty meal cooked over the fire, we held devotions and then crawled into our sleeping bags for a good night's rest. The whole week became one great adventure. On the day before our departure, my brother, the adventure leader/driver, planned to leave at daybreak and go caving in a fairly inaccessible spot.

The land cruiser was loaded with the necessary gear, and we all piled inside. The route into this particular valley was traversed by means of a rocky, potholed track. It was easily negotiated by the four-wheel drive with the subsequent swaying and pitching adding to the students' enjoyment. The views were spectacular and the silent remoteness thrilled the city kids unused to experiencing such a wild environment. After some hours, we reached an area with several caves, which my brother had previously explored.

By this time, we had experienced only one mishap with a girl spraining her ankle. However, she could still hobble, and she was allowed to enter the cave. We managed the narrow passageways and tight squeezes and also disturbed a smelly bat colony that vented their displeasure on intruders to their private territory.

When we stepped back into the broad daylight, every one of us was covered in gluey, red mud. We planned to wash and eat lunch further down where a stream meandered through the valley. Once we arrived by the river and freshened up, it was decided, after studying surveyor's maps, to let the group hike back up the mountain where we would pick them up several hours later. My husband and I, the driver, and the girl with the sprained ankle remained with the Land Cruiser, and we waved goodbye to the excited group with their filled water bottles. We knew we would reach the top long before them, so we relaxed and brewed tea. Then it was time to go.

The heavily loaded vehicle would not budge. Its weight had caused it to settle deep into the soft grassy ground next to the river. We weren't too worried because my brother was a practical guy, but after several attempts at starting the vehicle, he stopped, troubled by the possibility of flooding the engine.

His uncharacteristic anxiety gave us all cause for worry. What would happen to the group if we didn't turn up just before nightfall? After attempting to call them, we realized our cell phones were out of range. We guessed they would simply wait for us all night, or worse, they would make an attempt to find their way back to the farmhouse without flashlights. The weight of our responsibility weighed us down. How could we have been so naive?

My brother decided we would have to push the vehicle so he could clutch start the engine. We all grimaced at the prospect of two small people plus a girl with a swelling ankle pushing the weighty vehicle across the soft, level ground. But we tried and tried.

Nothing! It just sat there, totally immovable.

At that point, we knew nothing short of a miracle would get us out of there. We couldn't help but think of the point we had been trying to make all week—trusting the Lord in every situation in life. We believed it, and now it was time to prove our convictions. We prayed earnestly, acknowledging our helplessness and our heavenly Father's might. We asked the Lord for an angelic intervention. He already knew about our situation, and after all, He was in control of our lives and also those of the young people.

Feeling slightly foolish, but ready to put our faith to the test, the three of us got behind that stubborn, metal mountain again, prepared to exert our puny strength to the limit. We yelled, "Push!" at the top of our lungs and had barely laid our hands on it when it moved as if we were pushing a child's bicycle. Staring at each other in amazement, we laughed as the ponderous vehicle coasted with ease along the soft earth. We listened with astonishment as the engine roared to life.

We reached our students, eager to share what the Lord had done. Those challenging words from the eleventh chapter of Mark reminded us that our faith in God, combined with His power, could do wondrous things. To this day, we remember the seeming impossibility of the situation and how the Lord spared one of His unseen angels to give us that miraculous push.

—*Rita Stella Galieh*

The Peace
Offering

*But among you it will be different. Who-
ever wants to be a leader among you must
be your servant, and whoever wants to be
first among you must become your slave.*

Matthew 20:26–27

The plate of cookies Betty carried into the lunchroom may have been nothing special to the
average onlooker. But to those of us at the Colorado
Department of Agriculture, where I was doing the last
day of my summer internship, it was a momentous
event. To most of the group, those cookies were the
equivalent of blood from a turnip. To Betty, they were
a gift from the heart. To me, they were the most important accomplishment of my internship, because they
meant I had finally done something that mattered.

Betty was the first person everyone encountered
when they entered the office of the CDA. She sat

behind her particleboard desk, greeting guests and fellow employees alike with a resentful stare. Her round face rarely lifted in a smile. Even her graying curls were kept in check and not allowed to get out of line.

The first day on a new job is never very soothing, and Betty's icy gaze did little to welcome me as I hesitantly introduced myself. I flashed my best smile, determined to make a good impression. A long silence followed as Betty continued to stare at me. I wondered what to do next. Fortunately another coworker arrived and escorted me to my new desk. It was a rocky start.

Most of the other employees didn't even glance at Betty when they passed her desk on their way to their offices. Unless they had to deal directly with her, she did not exist. When they did have reasons to interact, I often overheard sharp words and angry exchanges. I listened to tirades of frustration from my office mates.

"Good morning, Betty," I said, week after week. Eventually she began to reply. In time, I discovered that the Wal-Mart frames behind her desk contained pictures of her children. One day, we happened to be coming from the musty elevator to the narrow door at the same time, and she nodded, without her usual stiff formality, when I held the door for her. She started thanking me for the extra work I did for her.

A summer filled with paperwork, bureaucracy, and education flew by. I discovered how the state works with farmers and other food production businesses to promote Colorado and advance agriculture. I escorted foreign businessmen on excursions to see American grocery stores. I processed paperwork and mailed out mountains of information. Of all the things I was learning, my relationship with Betty provided the greatest challenges—and the most significant rewards. Our morning greetings were friendly now, and my coworkers would watch without comment as Betty and I discussed the weather and what we had done over the weekend.

I knew progress was being made the day I was trying to finish a directory of local hay growers. The copy machine was old and belligerent, and while most days I could wrangle it, today I was making no headway. After about the fifth attempted restart, I slammed the lid a little harder than I intended. Betty looked up with a faint smile. She reached past me, flipped levers, moved knobs, and withdrew a mangled sheet of jammed paper. Then, she closed the lid, and the now submissive machine hummed with willingness.

"Wow," I said. "You really know how to make this thing work." She nodded and reached for my stack of papers. "Let me do those for you."

I knew better than to make a big deal of her offer. Gushing thanks would only bring out defensiveness. "Thanks, that's a great help," was all I said, but my heart was joyful.

A hesitant ceasefire developed in the office. Requests for Betty's help were now met with a short, but civil reply. The hostile comments about and toward her dwindled away. Things were not warm and easy, but they were professional.

My coworkers, who I had come to know and appreciate, planned to have a potluck on Friday for my last day. Everyone signed up to bring a little something, but Betty's name wasn't on the sheet. "Betty never brings anything," someone said. "She just takes our food back to her desk and eats there." I shrugged. It didn't matter to me if she brought anything, but I did want to be able to enjoy my last day without any office fireworks. Then, Thursday night, Betty's name appeared on the list with a note saying she would bring cookies.

Friday morning was filled with work, moments of laughter, and the bittersweet feelings that come with moving on from a familiar and comfortable place. As the time for our potluck arrived, we gathered in the lunchroom. Wonderful smells of green chili and beans, burritos, and tacos made my stomach grumble with impatience. I looked around, but Betty was not there. A quick trip to her desk revealed she had gone. I must have looked disappointed because when I returned to the lunchroom, my friend Laura put her arm around me. "We'll have more fun without her!" she said.

"I really thought she would be here," I replied.

Laura shook her head. "She'll never change."

Lunch was delicious, and I felt warmed by the kind wishes from my friends and summer mentors. Still, I was a bit hurt by Betty's absence. I really thought she had started to like me. Suddenly, she walked through the lunchroom door with her plate of cookies. "I had to run clear out to my car to get these and wait for some idiot who was holding up the elevator," she announced in a loud voice. At that moment, my whole day turned sunny.

By serving Betty, I not only earned her trust and affection, but also earned appreciation and admiration from my coworkers. When I treated Betty with respect and kindness, I facilitated a change I never anticipated. God granted me the blessing of being a peacemaker. I left my internship content, knowing I had accomplished something over the summer that would continue to reward me long after graduation.

—*Melanie Platt*

I Wish I May,
I Wish I Might

*Take delight in the Lord, and he will
give you your heart's desires.*

Psalm 37:4

I sat in my tiny apartment in Tokyo, Japan, and fingered the promise engraved on my best friend's wedding program—one of the few mementos I brought with me. Linda, so happy and sure of her future, had been given the desires of *her* heart. Where did I go wrong? I had been a Christian since accepting Christ at vacation Bible school at age five, and I counseled kids at our church camp for five summers, but I felt as far away from the fulfillment of this verse's promise as I was from my mother's home in Ohio.

I knew what some of my desires were, and none of them were working out very well. I wanted my old boyfriend Dale back, but I knew in my heart we would never repair our broken relationship. Was Tokyo far enough away to allow my emotions the space and time needed to catch up to that reality? I hoped so. I thought I wanted to teach middle school history; so how did I end up in this international school classroom of five-year-old children, where English was a second language for most, and there was a dictatorial nun for a principal? Did she really expect these non–English-speaking children to be reading *Dr. Seuss* by Christmas? That was only a couple of months away, and the class still met my questions with blank stares. I was terrified I would fail, but I didn't see any other conclusion.

Everything had gone terribly wrong, and I had the sinking feeling it had something to do with the first part of that verse. Did I "take delight in the Lord?" I wasn't even sure what that meant, but I became determined to find out. Once I did, perhaps God would fulfill His promise, and like my friend, Linda, I would be blessed with the desires of my heart.

I began by taking a hard look at the state of my faith fundamentals.

Prayer life—panicky, pleading cries for help. I didn't believe God would really do something about my situation, and I didn't thank Him for what He was doing already, because I frankly couldn't see what He was doing.

Church attendance—spotty since arriving in Japan. I needed to pick one of the English-speaking churches in Tokyo and attend regularly.

Study of God's Word—did I remember to pack my Bible? Must be around here someplace.

Obedience—time for honesty again. Fitting in to the social life at the school and not making too many mistakes in the Japanese culture (it's rude to refuse the beer that keeps getting poured at dinners out, right?) seemed a clearer daily priority than figuring out what God wanted me to do.

Grade: D– (As a Harvard graduate, I was too proud to give myself an F.)

Where had my faith gone? As a camp counselor, I depended on God and found Him faithful in helping me to deal with cabin situations. He had been with me through my parents' divorce and helped me to forgive their mistakes. When had my faith become so precarious?

Of course, I knew the answer to that question. Between a Japanese boyfriend in graduate school who questioned every aspect of my faith, and time spent at a church with some rather suspicious doctrine, I had let doubts erode my once-firm foundation. While in graduate school, I actually applied through my denomination to go as a short-term missionary to Japan the following year. By the end of the school year, I called to withdraw my name. I no longer felt I could go ask other people to draw closer to Jesus when I felt so far from His side.

Suddenly I felt shaky in every aspect of my life. The principal questioned every move I made in the classroom, and I started to doubt my ability to teach. I had no idea why I wanted to go to Japan in the first place. What was I doing there? Where did I belong? My friends had seemed to know exactly where to go and what to do after graduation, but my itchy feet had led me to seek adventure. Now, I just felt lost.

By Christmas, I was not only lost, but also sick and home in bed with a very high fever and no aspirin. I spent the two-week vacation crying, savoring the Swedish pepperkakor cookies that a friend sent me, and gazing at my ten-inch-tall evergreen "tree" in a pot I had decorated with the Uncle Sam and American flag ornaments my mom had sent me. She had no doubts as to where I belonged. I was miserable.

Well, the kids in my classroom were not reading *Dr. Seuss* by Christmas, but imperceptibly, miraculously, most of them *could* read by February. One day Akimasa couldn't read, and the next day he could! I took no credit, but thanked God that the kids were now reading in spite of my lack of experience and the depth of my unhappiness. One day, a visitor to my classroom made the observation that while I was with the children, I actually looked very happy. I realized that even though I had been so ill-prepared to teach five-year-olds, I had grown to love them. They were simply adorable.

Imperceptibly, miraculously, my "faith fundamentals" program was also working. My church attendance was not only much better, but also the pastor somehow designed every sermon around my spiritual needs! I frequently looked over my shoulder to see if anyone could tell that the pastor seemed to have a portal to my soul. I joined a Bible study and discovered the wonders of a study Bible. Who knew you could read a verse about the Egyptian slave masters who oppressed the Israelites and then follow that up by learning about slave masters depicted on wall paintings in Theban tombs—just by looking at the bottom of the page?

I found myself humming the hymns I had been brought up on while walking to and from school. I began talking to God constantly. I realized that just because drinking beer was a pervasive part of every meal in Japan, I could actually say "kekkou desu," meaning "no, thanks, I'm fine." I clung to God's presence. I had never needed Him so much in my life, and I discovered He was always with me. By the time the cherry blossoms were in full bloom, I knew exactly what I was doing in Japan. God had brought me there so I could hear Him better.

I stayed in Japan for two more years, and by the time I left, I wanted nothing more than to serve the God I now loved so much. He led me home to Seattle. I went there without a job and my best friend in Seattle was now married and gone to Minnesota, but I was so caught up in the exhilaration of following God's will that I frequently caught myself speeding on the highways. I knew I had received the ultimate desire of my heart—faith in a God who loved me, and who held me securely in the palm of His hand.

—*Sonja M. Anderson*

Without
My Help

*And my God will meet all your needs accord-
ing to his glorious riches in Christ Jesus.*

Philippians 4:19

My husband, Gordon, had only one thing to
say after losing his job as a design engineer:
"Thank you, Lord!" He had wanted to quit for several months, but the Lord encouraged him to wait.
He accepted the offered severance package, which
would not have been an option had he resigned. To
make ends meet while he looked for other employment, we started our own business. We worked as
an independent contractor in jobs that ranged from
home repair and remodeling to staffing a wilderness
base camp for troubled teens.

After two years of searching for a regular job,
resulting in only three interviews and zero job offers,

we were near the end of our savings. We knew something else needed to happen. A close friend in the northeastern part of Texas told us about someone he knew who was hiring. Before our money was completely gone, we made plans to drive from Oregon to Texas. The terrorist attacks on September 11, 2001 delayed us about three weeks, but after things settled a little, we loaded our travel trailer and headed out, stopping along the way to check on other potential employment.

By the time we arrived in East Texas, the work we had heard about was gone. Gordon used our friend's computer to access the Internet, and within two weeks he had applied, interviewed, and accepted a good job in Henderson. I flew back to Oregon. Gordon started his new position the first week in November. He and our dog, a lab/retriever cross, lived in the travel trailer parked at our friend's business.

At home once again, my challenges also began. The house we owned in Oregon wasn't in any shape to sell. We had started a remodeling project the day we bought it, and five years later, we weren't finished. Gordon flew home for the holidays, enclosed the utility room, and installed a new shower. He came again over Memorial Day, took care of a few details on the house, loaded a truck with stuff from his shop, and drove it back to Texas.

While he tackled a different application of his engineering skills, I learned to tape and patch sheet-rock and apply texture. A girlfriend and I installed a new toilet that even worked. My mom and I painted the kitchen and cleaned. I sorted, packed, sold some things, gave other items away, and hauled stuff to the dump. My dad and I installed light fixtures and ceiling fans. Finally, I put the house on the market and waited.

In spite of the pitiful housing market in our part of Oregon, several potential buyers came to look. A young couple with two boys expressed sincere interest. Their house had been on the market with no prospective buyers in sight. We accepted their offer, subject to the sale of their house, and waited once more. Of course, I packed while we waited, spent precious time with my family, and completed little details that needed to be finished. Nothing happened.

Gordon and I wanted to resume our life together and waited for the house to sell so we could move on with our plans. I kept telling myself how limited my mortal view was, and I remembered that God's time-table is not mine. But when our plans continued to feel as if they were frozen in time, I began to wonder if God was ignoring our needs and desires. Even though I knew it wasn't true, I felt lonely and unloved.

In the middle of my frustration, the Lord whispered to my heart: *I can sell the house without you here and without your help. You need to be with Gordon, not apart from him.*

I realized that instead of doing what we should do—be together regardless—we had allowed an economic situation, not within our control, to dictate our circumstances.

As a result, I reached a decision the middle of August. "Find us a place to rent," I told Gordon. "I'm moving even though the house hasn't sold."

Less than two weeks later, he arrived to help. We loaded the dog I'd recently acquired, the cat, and our belongings into a large truck, two trailers, and my SUV. A flat tire on one of the trailers near Jerome, Idaho, delayed us. "I'm sure glad you noticed the low tire when we were getting fuel," Gordon said.

"Thank the Lord we didn't have to stop along the highway somewhere to wait while it was fixed," I replied with a deep sigh.

The moving truck's fastest speed, downhill, was only fifty-five miles per hour. As if our progress wasn't slow enough already, I took the wrong road off the exit and had to backtrack several miles the opposite direction to access the interstate again in the right direction. When we finally reached the campground we had found listed in our directory, the manager told us the cabins were closed after Labor Day for the winter, even though the directory failed to note it. Our plans to stop for the day before dark foiled, we continued on toward Price, Utah. Somewhere along the way, I received a call on my cell phone.

It was the young woman who had contracted to buy our house. "Nanci, this is Yvette. We've got a buyer for our house."

"Wonderful!" I couldn't wait to tell Gordon. "Yvette, I'm driving at the moment. I need to call you back when we get to Price, so I can jot down the information and take some notes."

"I'll be here. Just call," she said.

We didn't make it to Price. In the middle of nowhere, the tail and running lights on the moving truck stopped working—not the safest thing to happen in the dark. We found the only rest area between Provo and Price and stopped. Gordon tried in vain to figure out the light problem while I discovered I had no cell phone service, whatsoever. However, the rest area had a working pay phone, and I had a flashlight. Yvette and I connected and she gave me the information she had.

God waited patiently for me to finally leave things in His hands and allow him to meet our needs. He only needed my willingness to listen and be obedient. Yes, the Lord can and did sell the house without me being there. My obedience produced faith, or did my faith produce obedience? Either way, God met our needs, on *His* time, without my help, and in spite of setbacks in other areas.

The problem with the lights did not get resolved that night. Before we could take advantage of the futon mattress we'd placed in the back of my SUV, we had to remove all the stuff we'd packed from my vehicle and stash it around the cat's carrier in the front seat of the moving truck and on the ground by the trailer. Preparations accomplished, Gordon climbed into the back of the SUV to get some rest. On the way, he bumped the alarm on the key ring and the horn began to blow. We found humor in the situation, but I doubt the people nearby, awakened by the noise, were amused. After things grew quiet again, we snuggled together to get some sleep.

"We have a comfy bed, water, food, our dog and cat, and each other. What more do we need?" I asked.

"Not a thing," Gordon replied.

As my eyelids grew heavy, I whispered a prayer. "Thank you, Lord for Your divine protection, Your help, Your love, and Your sense of humor."

—*Nanci G. Huyser*

They Know Not
What They Do

My health may fail, and my spirit may grow weak,
but God remains the strength of my heart;
He is mine forever.

Psalm 73:26

The morning was bright, and the sun warmed us in our elementary school's annual field day. A sense of excitement fueled our three-legged races, sack hops, and eggs carried on spoons over finish lines. "Go, Daddy Long-Legs!" shouted my friend, Paul, as I sprinted past him in the fifty-yard dash. The wind was like water against my face, lifting and lowering my ponytail flowing behind me, pushing me gently on. I didn't think of the winning of each race as much as the feeling inside when I ran. I was like a cantering horse; every muscle moved in sync, giving me an incredible feeling of joy.

It was after we had a special race in gym class—fourth graders against fifth—that the trouble began. On that day, I beat the fastest fifth-grader, a handsome, intelligent boy who didn't realize that his looks alone made him outstanding. Tony turned to me when we lined up to go back to class. "So, you think you're faster than me."

A small twinge of fear rippled through me when I saw his face. My older brother, Rick, would get the same look when I practiced acrobatics in our living room when our parents were out. It was when they weren't home that Rick sometimes hit me. "You think you're better than me?" he demanded. Sometimes, the names he called me hurt just as much: stupid, ugly, and failure. Sometimes, even when he wasn't there, my fear returned, bringing his words into my head until they crowded out everything else. It was like being punched over and over by an invisible foe. The worst part was that the fear transformed his words into something I was slowly beginning to believe.

Somehow, I looked Tony in the eye and said, "No. I *know* I'm faster." He looked surprised, but said nothing more.

The school day ended, and as I walked down the hallway, I began to feel as though I was teetering on a cliff. Now, the wind didn't ruffle my hair with playfulness but threatened to push me over the edge.

Today was the first time I'd ever spoken up for myself. *What's going to happen to me now?* I wondered.

When I passed the principal's office, the hallway suddenly dimmed into muted grays.

What's going on? I thought. I stared hard at the electric, white outline of a woman in front of me. I strained to peer through the growing darkness, my eyes not leaving her shape as it moved down the hall. *If I can just follow her, I'll make it outside,* I told myself.

I heard my classmate, Lisa, but could see nothing. "Hey, Christine, watch it! What are you doing?" She sounded a bit annoyed. Sunlight broke through my blindness then, and I saw that I had bumped head-long into her, knocking off her crossing guard helmet and stopping short of stumbling into the afternoon traffic. The outline of the woman, I realized, had long vanished. I tried to kneel down. I never felt my face hit the ground.

Mama picked me up after school. I awoke, lying on the back seat of her station wagon, alone. I watched the last of the students find their rides and tried to remember what had happened. "Mrs. Dorton said you fainted because you ran too fast in gym." Mama got in behind the wheel. "How are you feeling now?"

"Okay." *But I didn't faint right after gym,* I thought. *It was later, when I'd felt really scared.* But I didn't tell

Mama that. I just watched the clouds through the window, all the way home.

The next day, gym class began as usual: runner's stretches, arm swings, and jumping jacks. Coach Eanes turned to me when we were done. "You aren't allowed to run anymore, Christine. Go over and sit by the stage and wait for the class to finish."

I'm not allowed to run? Forever? I felt disappointment and a rush of shame as I walked to the steps, hidden behind a wall. I thought of field day, with the wind gently pushing me on. *I don't want to cry, I don't want to cry,* I thought, but tears fell onto my hands clenched below. We'd learned that God hears us even when we don't think He's listening. *He can't be listening now,* I thought to myself.

At lunch, my best friend, Dana, sat her tray down next to mine. "Tony asked me if I thought you'd go out with him. I told him no, but that I would talk to you about it."

I shrugged, brushing away the hurt. Dana wasn't acting like my friend. Why did Tony like me when I couldn't run?

Our class headed to Mass. As Father Lou recited the opening prayers, my mind focused on the cross above the altar. Jesus' head was slumped to one side, his fingers limp beneath the point where his hands had been nailed. *Such bad things happened to Him,* I thought. But, even though some people hated him, He taught them to turn the other cheek. *I don't understand, Jesus. You should have fought back. People just hurt you again unless you fight back.*

"Lord, have mercy," Father Lou was praying.

"Lord, have mercy," we echoed.

"Christ, have mercy."

Sister Helen taught us that afternoon why Jesus had died on the cross. He forgave us because He loved us, enough to give up His life for our sins. *Jesus was turning His other cheek when He died on the cross,* I thought. *But He didn't have to. He could've fought any enemy and won.*

After school, I climbed into the cradle of two branches in my favorite oak tree at home, a place where I felt safe and able to breathe again. I thought of Jesus and the cross and closed my eyes. "Dear God," I prayed. "I don't like being afraid of Rick, and I wish we could be friends. But I just don't know how. And now, I can't run and, well, could you please tell me what to do?" I suddenly remembered Sister Helen's lesson. One of the last things Jesus had done was ask His Father to forgive his enemies. "For they know not what they do." It dawned on me: I needed to love Rick enough to forgive him. *Maybe,* I thought, *things would be better if I could just forgive him.*

The next spring, Baba registered us for the town's first soccer league. A slight wind rippled our shirts, and the field was streaked with shadows and sunlight on the day of our first game. I had the position of halfback, meaning I needed to sprint in every direction to help both offense and defense. I looked over at the sidelines, where my mother, father and sister stood. Beside them, Rick was clapping. "Go, Christine!" he yelled, with all his might.

I ran as hard and as fast as I could, dribbling the ball around opposing players. With God's help, the fear and hatred were gone. In their place were a joy and feeling of freedom that we could love each other as brother and sister. The ball shot into the net at the end of the field, and my teammates and I jumped up and down, hugging each other.

Since that time, I have strived toward the goal of doing my best in whatever position God has given me and loving my brothers and sisters in Christ enough to help them in any way I can. Forgiveness is a way to love not only our enemies, but also ourselves. If we all do this, if we all work together in love, we can't help but win the game.

—*Christine P. Wang*

A Thorny Rose

*The Lord says, "I will guide you along the
best pathway for your life. I will advise
you and watch over you. Do not be like
a senseless horse or mule that needs a bit
and bridle to keep it under control."*

Psalm 32:8–9

Dust rose in a cloud behind my boyfriend's
twelve-year-old station wagon as he turned
down the dirt road leading to the Rocking E Ranch.
I smiled at Stan and then glanced in the backseat
where Andrea chatted with Rickey. Only a phone
call from my equine-loving girlfriend could have
dragged us all from bed on a Saturday morning to go
horseback riding. As we piled from the car, the sun
beat down on our heads even though it was just ten

o'clock. Several horses stood listlessly near a fence in competition for the shade from a massive oak tree. It was going to be a scorcher for early June.

Andrea approached two men saddling a light gray mare. "We'd like to rent four horses."

After we paid our fees, the ranch hands chose mounts for Andrea, Stan, and Rickey. Then it was my turn. One of the men eyed me closely. "Have you ridden before?"

"Yes," I replied honestly. After all, I rode Andrea's gentle quarter horse whenever she and I visited the barn where she boarded him. Then, last summer, Stan and I had gone on two trail rides, perched on docile horses that followed one another around a beaten path.

The man nodded toward the gray mare. "All right, Johnny, give her Rose." I caught a glimpse of the grin that accompanied his order and wondered at its meaning.

When they brought the horse over, I patted her neck. *Rose. Did they name you that because you're so sweet?* Somehow I doubted it. Rose stood still as Johnny helped me into the saddle. Despite my insistent nudges to her flanks, she continued to stand still while Andrea and the boys started off down the wide gravel road leading to the trail. I looked at my tennis shoes and wished for bona fide cowboy boots like Andrea's, something a horse could actually feel.

"Give her a good kick," Johnny instructed and slapped her rump. Rose walked a few feet, turned, and headed back toward the shade. No amount of pulling on the reins could convince her to do otherwise. Johnny caught the bridle and adjusted the bit in her mouth. "You've got to hold the reins tight," he instructed. "If she gets the bit between her teeth, you can't control her. She has a mind of her own." I saw Johnny's boss smirk.

The ranch hand gave Rose another smack, and we started forward. Rose danced around for several yards with both of us struggling for control of the bit. She would turn to the right, and I would pull to the left. Then she would turn to the left, and I would pull to the right. Eventually, Rose won, and she circled back to the laughing men again.

Johnny made another adjustment, and Rose and I took off again. We struggled for a few moments, but this time it looked as if I had gained the upper hand in our battle for the bit. Rose seemed to accept the inevitable and slipped into a steady trot. After a few minutes, I relaxed a little and began to enjoy the ride. About three quarters of a mile down the road, I looked for my friends who were nowhere in sight. *Oh, well. We'll catch up with them.* I eased back in the saddle.

Suddenly, Rose made a sharp turn to the left and headed toward a small pond in a thicket of pine trees. I hauled on the reins as hard as I could and yelled, "Whoa!" in my best cowboy voice. It always worked in the movies, but apparently Rose didn't watch the same movies I did. Her pace never slowed, and we headed straight for the pond.

As my mule-headed mount stepped into the water, I frantically tried to kick free of the stirrups so I could pull my legs up and avoid getting my pants and shoes wet. It was too late. The pond had very little slope, and we sank right in, the water as high as Rose's shoulder. There we sat, my pants soaked halfway up my thighs. "All right, you stupid horse!" I yelled. "I can sit here as long as you can." Rose twitched her ears, unconcerned.

It took several minutes for the angry red mists to clear from my eyes, but when they did, I assessed my situation. The tiny "pond" looked more like a deserted watering hole. Aquatic vegetation choked the steep sides. Towering pines, overgrown with honeysuckle and poison ivy, made the area dark and creepy. As I looked into the murky water, I realized this would be the perfect habitat for water moccasins!

I pulled furiously on the reins in an attempt to induce Rose to abandon her game, but to no avail. "You can stay in this snake pit if you want," I shouted, "but I'm getting out of here." I turned and slid across her hindquarters to the edge of the pond. My sodden pants, now complete with a layer of mud, weighed a ton as I stood up and began the trek back to Stan's station wagon. I fumed as I marched along, my shoes sloshing with each step. *Well, they sure named you right, Rose, only you're a rose full of thorns. You could have got me killed with that malicious stunt. Oh, why did I ever come horseback riding in the first place?*

That horse had not only put me into danger, but she also could have become a snakebite victim, too, all because she didn't want to go for a trail ride. She was obstinate, headstrong, willful, and . . . then I stopped. How many times had my stubbornness taken me into deep waters? How often had my pride put me into danger? I thought about the countless occasions when I had fought God for control of my life and cringed. Was He trying to teach me something through the antics of a stiff-necked horse? Maybe Rose and I were more alike than I wanted to admit. Maybe I needed to hand the reins back over to God and let Him lead for a change.

I walked a few more feet when I heard Rose splash her way onto dry land. She galloped triumphantly past me and headed toward her shady spot by the fence. I shook my head and chuckled. *A Rose by any other name would be . . . me!*

—Tracy Crump

From Panic
to Peace

So be strong and courageous! Do not be afraid
and do not panic before them. For the Lord
your God will personally go ahead of you.
He will neither fail you nor abandon you.

Deuteronomy 31:6

I t was a time full of difficult, almost overwhelming
circumstances in my life. My teenage son had been
going through some very rebellious years, finances
were tight, and my marriage was in deep trouble. I
felt quite alone in my role as a single mother. On one
particular hot summer night in 1992, I discovered I
wasn't alone at all. I realized that, through prayer,
I could talk to God about anything, and He would
guide me through the turmoil. He would keep his
promises.

My seventeen-year-old son, Shawn, was spending this otherwise typical day with his friend, Kerry, at an amusement park about an hour-and-a-half drive from our home. I knew the park closed at 10:00 and didn't expect him to be home until around 11:30, or at least soon after. Despite our recent problems, Shawn was becoming quite responsible in returning home when expected. Tired from a stressful day at my job, I had gone to bed where I offered a quick prayer for their safety and then dozed off, at peace with the world.

At midnight, I woke up with an overpowering sense that something was wrong. I jumped out of bed and rushed to Shawn's room, hoping that he had returned home and that my overwhelming feeling of dread was nothing more than a frazzled Mom's overactive imagination. When I opened the door and saw the empty room and untouched bed, my heart sank. The boys weren't that late, but I felt certain they were in danger.

I paced the floor as I cried out to God. Abruptly, I felt a powerful urge to kneel and pray for Shawn and Kerry's safety. I pleaded with the Lord to deliver them safely home, remembering and thanking him for the many times in the past he had saved Shawn from troubling and even dangerous circumstances. The sense of danger and need to pray did not pass for what seemed to be a very long time, but was probably only twenty minutes or so. After the prayers and much agonizing, I was extremely tired, but very much at peace. I laid my head on the pillow and fell asleep immediately.

Soon after, I was awakened again, this time by my son poking his head into my bedroom. "Mom, Mom, you awake? I'm sorry I'm late, but you won't believe what happened to us tonight."

I glanced at the clock and realized that nearly an hour and a half had passed since I'd gone back to bed. Now wide awake, I went limp with relief at the sight of my son now safe at home. "Of course, I'll believe you," I said. "Tell me everything!"

For the second time that night, I got out of bed and listened intently as Shawn described the events of the evening. After leaving the park, Kerry and he had missed a turn on their way to the interstate and become lost. They ended up in a disreputable part of town, one that was especially dangerous at that time of night. They didn't know what else to do, so they stopped at an all-night service station to get directions back to the interstate.

While Kerry went in, Shawn waited in the car, and as he looked around, he noticed two suspicious looking characters: one at a pay phone and one standing alone looking quite nervous. Both men were staring in Shawn's direction, but he tried to avoid eye contact and looked the other way. He locked his door, although one window was still partially open. Sure enough, the nervous looking man approached the car where the window was down and peering inside started pressuring Shawn with some questions. He tried to open one of the locked car doors, but just then Kerry came out of the station and, oblivious to any danger, brushed past the stranger and got into the driver's seat.

One glance at Shawn's ashen face and he knew something was up. By this time, the second man was off the phone and a third man had appeared from around a dark corner of the building, joining the other two. All three men were now standing around the car, looking quite threatening and making it impossible to leave. One of them asked Shawn and Kerry if they would help push their car around the back of the building, into what looked to be a dark alley.

The boys were terrified—afraid to say no, afraid to say yes. They feared the rough-looking men might be armed. "We had no idea what was going to happen," Shawn said, still obviously shaken by the incident.

Then, God created an unexpected moment of opportunity for Shawn and Kerry. The three men began discussing something, and that brief opening allowed Kerry to start the car and race out of the parking lot. Miraculously, the boys escaped unharmed, and they were finally on their way home.

Something occurred to me while Shawn was talking. I realized that my fearful awakening at midnight and my intense petitions for the boys' safety occurred at almost the exact time of their terrifying experience. In addition, their moment of opportunity and subsequent escape coincided with my feelings of peace and release from praying.

It was then Shawn and I understood how God had intervened to protect Kerry and him. Only God knew both sides of the situation: a mom fearing for her son's safety and the impending danger two boys faced. I'm so thankful that he used me to intervene and, in the process, calmed my fearful heart. Indeed, there would be more trying circumstances to come in our lives, but this was a moment of knowing, without a doubt, that God's promises were true. Deuteronomy 31:6 became more than just a Bible verse that day. It became words to live by—an amazing promise from an amazing God.

—*Beverly Rothgery*

Editing Matters

If you need wisdom, ask our gener-
ous God, and He will give it to you.
He will not rebuke you for asking.

James 1:5

I had just finished scratching comments on twenty-four freshman papers. My back ached and my eyes burned. I glanced at the clock. It was 5:29. "I should be on my way home," I mumbled and picked up the next paper. I clicked the plastic pencil, lengthening the lead, when I noticed a stranger in the doorway. *I hope this guy's not looking for me to edit something,* I thought. *I'm edited out.*

I stood up and held out my hand. "How can I help you?" My words fell like a paperweight. *Way to make a good first impression,* my mind lectured.

"I was wondering if I could have a few minutes of your time?" He stared at the old Windsor next to my desk.

"Sure. Have a seat." I motioned to the chair. "How's your day been?" I asked in an attempt to redeem myself.

"It's been nice. You have a lot of friendly people on this campus." He glanced over my bookshelves, as if studying their contents. "I'm not just saying this to be polite," he continued. "Even the students have stopped to talk to me. You must have a very selective admissions process." His stare questioned me as he leaned forward in the chair. A heavy curiosity narrowed his eyes and pursed the corners of his mouth.

That's when I realized this conversation wasn't about editing. It wasn't even about the college's admissions process or the friendly students. Instead, it was about this man, this stranger who sat in the old, wooden chair next to my desk.

"We do have a discerning policy," I said.

"Is that because you're all religious?"

Although my religious sensitivities stirred a bit, I knew that discussing the role of religion would do little to meet the real need waiting behind his question. I remembered James's admonition, "If you need wisdom . . . ask Him, and He will gladly tell you."

I quietly asked God to help me find the words that would help this man find Him—and the words came.

The stranger and I explored plays like Beckett's *Waiting for Godot*. We talked about the futility of waiting for someone, especially a savior, who never comes. And then we talked about Jesus. We discussed the ambiguities in the titles of plays, like Pirandello's *Six Characters in Search of an Author*, where the characters search for a creator they never find. Then, we talked about God. We worked through C. S. Lewis's insights and his questions about the source of each human being's innate sense of good. We discussed God's desire for us to experience His best.

Fifty minutes later, after playing a kind of intellectual ping-pong with philosophy and literature, we moved away from the constant theme of emptiness in human experience and the ugly realities of sin in a postmodern world. Finally, we talked about the gospel. We talked about our need for a savior, Christ's amazing demonstration of love on the cross, and the power and reality of the resurrection.

The conversation turned in one direction, then another. Each trail started to lead us away from where I thought we should be heading, but suddenly I'd find him asking another question that led us back to the only real answer—Jesus and our need for his forgiveness. Sometimes, we headed up what I thought would be insurmountable hills of philosophy, but we always made it down the other side together.

He didn't indicate any commitment to follow Christ there in my office, but he did thank me for the conversation. "Maybe we could have lunch the next time I stop by. I really have appreciated this opportunity." He smiled and held out his hand. "I took a class on Christianity once, but my professor never talked about any of this. Thanks for taking the time."

After he left, I closed the door. I sat down in the same wooden chair the visitor had occupied only moments before. I stared at the plethora of papers and the plastic pencils and then at the door. I thanked God for taking the time to edit my grumpy attitude and nearsighted disposition. I thanked Him for the college writing papers that kept me at my desk that afternoon. Finally, I thanked him for answering my prayer for wisdom with the surprising words He helped me form as I talked with this stranger.

As I drifted back over the conversation, I was stunned by the road of words we had traveled and how carefully God helped me navigate each turn and hill. Then the weight and privilege of God's promise hit me. He had given me more than the wisdom I requested. The Lord had chosen to use a simple writing teacher, a tired professor with a poor attitude, to help edit what might become a new chapter for this stranger—a chapter in a book called *Eternity.*

—*Marty Trammell*

Do Angels Drive Pickups?

For he will order his angels
to protect you wherever you go.

Psalm 91:11

There were just a few of us who braved the downpour that spring night to attend prayer meeting at our little church in a central Canadian city. None of us even noticed the pickup with the different license plate parked out front. We were surprised, therefore, when a stranger came through the door behind us. A tall, lanky fellow carrying a well-worn Bible, he introduced himself as Ed. "Just traveling through on my way to the West Coast." The West Coast was 1,400 miles away.

We welcomed him into the circle of prayer, but I noticed him shuffling uneasily when the leader asked if there were any specific requests. Finally Ed spoke up. "I'm in a bit of a bind. This morning I lost my wallet with all my credit cards, and I need them to buy gas, so I can get home in time for work day after tomorrow. Maybe you'd pray that my wallet would turn up?"

This guy certainly had more faith than I did. To me, the chances of finding a lost wallet in a city of half a million people seemed impossible. *And where would he stay? And what would he eat?* I'll admit the thought of hosting a stranger did not seem particularly appealing at the moment. Our guest room was messy, the fridge all but depleted of leftovers.

"If you can just spare some money for gas, I'll be on my way right after prayers," Ed said. "I expect to drive all night, but I could sure do with a bite to eat. Haven't had anything since last night."

Well, that means I won't have to clean up my sewing scraps in the guest room, but let's see. I think I have eggs and a few potatoes I could fry.

"All right, then," the leader said. "Let's each pray and, afterward, we'll see what we can do to help Ed on his way."

I had a hard time concentrating. *Was this fellow just another con artist trying to bilk a few gullible people out of some cash? Yet, listen to him pray, so fluently and so sincerely.* When prayer time ended, we pooled our cash resources—only forty-five dollars. *But that sure*

won't buy him enough gas to get to the West Coast. And
what will he eat?

"Why don't you follow us home?" I heard myself
say. "It's not out of your way, and I'll make some supper for you." Now what have I done? This guy might
mug us both, steal us poor, and take off!

To my surprise, my husband, Leo, even volun-
teered to ride with Ed to show him the way.

Good grief! What if Ed takes him hostage and I
have to fork over ransom?

Despite the pelting rain, I managed to keep an
eye on their headlights in my rear view mirror all
the way home. As Ed and Leo visited, I fried potatoes and eggs, brewed some coffee, and buttered four
slices of toast. Ed wolfed it all down. "Have you got a
piano?" he asked.

"Yes, sure, it's in the family room downstairs,"
Leo replied. "Do you play?"

"A little," Ed replied.

I just hope this isn't some kind of sinister plot to get
Leo downstairs. I better find the cordless phone, just in
case. Strains of "Amazing Grace" and "Great Is Thy
Faithfulness" soon filtered up the stairwell, and then
I heard Ed saying, "Well I really must be on my way."
I breathed a sigh of relief.

"Guess what?" Leo said as he went for Ed's jacket.
"Ed lives in the same town on the West Coast as our

son, so he left me his address. Maybe they can get acquainted." Ed shook hands with us, thanked us for our hospitality, and drove off into the night in his pickup.

"You know, I really can't make up my mind about this guy," I said. "Have you got that address he gave you? I want to check it out."

I dialed the long distance operator, gave her Ed's name and address, and waited. "I'm sorry," she finally replied. "We have nobody here by that name."

"I think we've been taken," I said as I hung up the phone.

"Or maybe we've just entertained an angel unawares," Leo suggested.

"Not unless angels have unlisted numbers," I added in a voice full of sarcasm. "And doesn't the Bible refer to angels as 'ministering spirits?' Just what has Ed done for us, besides relieving us of some cash and emptying my fridge of leftovers?"

Strangely enough, after Ed's visit, instead of asking God to "bless so and so and send someone to provide their needs," I started asking myself, *am I that someone?*

Then there was that matter about "being given to hospitality." After reading about Jesus and His disciples making preparations for the Passover, the Lord's question, "Where is my guest room?" stuck with me.

After hosting Ed, it was as if Jesus was putting that very same question to me whenever I saw someone with a need. I began swallowing my pride and opening my home to give what I had, just as it was, right when it was needed, and not only when I was prepared.

As for my nagging mistrust of strangers, no doubt stoked by media efforts to warn people about scam artists, Ed's visit had actually reinforced my trust in God's protection, reminding me that most strangers are *not* out to harm me.

Ed may have emptied my fridge, but he filled me with the understanding that prayer often meant "share." He invoked some fears, but he also reinforced my sense of God's protection. He relieved me of some cash, but he also taught me greater compassion. He has remained a mystery, but he clearly showed me that hospitality is a must. Having taught me all that, who's to say Ed wasn't a "ministering spirit"?

Up until that point, I had always considered guardian angels purely in terms of the physical protection they offer in times of emergency. After Ed's visit, however, I realized I had been drifting slowly away from some of the Christian principles I should have been following. In one memorable evening, Ed brought my soul back on course.

—*Alma Barkman*

New York
Calling

You guide me with your counsel,
leading me to a glorious destiny.

Psalm 73:24

Growing up in Ohio was nice, but a little dull. Most of my friends intended to live there forever, but when I was in junior high, I remember sitting on my front porch and looking east with a dream of living in New York. Of course, at the time, I didn't realize New York meant rivers, mountains, and rural areas in addition to the city. Looking back, I think God implanted this dream in my heart even before I really knew Him.

When I was in the seventh grade, I often baby-sat for neighbors who were devout Christians. They often talked to me about their faith, and they had many Biblical books on their coffee table. "Feel free to read and relax after the children are in bed," they told me, and one evening I did just that. After putting the children to bed, I read a story about a gangster named Jim Vaus who had worked for Mickey Cohen, another gangster who made many headlines. Jim Vaus became a Christian during a Billy Graham Crusade, and I wept as I read how his life changed. A few weeks later I, too, committed my life to the Lord.

High school came and went, and soon, I entered Georgetown College, a small school located in the beautiful bluegrass area of Kentucky. Toward the end of my junior year, I was strolling across campus one morning when an announcement caught my eye. Jim Vaus was scheduled to speak on campus that evening. I remembered the article I read years ago, and I quickly found a pencil and scribbled down the building and room number.

That evening, I was sitting in the front row. Jim Vaus rose from his seat and stood right in front of me. "I'd like to tell you about a ministry of mine in New York called Youth Development Incorporated. We work with teenagers in Spanish Harlem. In summer, we take them to a camp in the Catskill Mountains in upstate New York, and I'm here to recruit summer staff to work with these kids." I learned the staff would spend two weeks in the city and then two weeks at camp, and then the cycle would be repeated.

My jaw dropped as I realized the opportunity before me. Was it possible my old dream of going to New York would come true? When the meeting ended, I picked up an employment application and walked slowly back to my dorm. "You won't believe what just happened," I told my roommate. I shared my dream with her, and soon, she was excited too. I could hardly sleep that night. I prayed about it, and two days later I dropped my application in the mail. I just *knew* I would be living my dream.

The semester drew to a close quickly. "Are you going to New York?" my roommate asked.

"I hope so, but I'm not sure," I said as I packed my bags. I hadn't heard back from Youth Development Incorporated. At home, my parents were glad to see me, but then I heard the question I knew was coming.

"What are your summer plans? Do you have a job lined up? If not, you'd better get on the stick and start applying," my mother said. "It's getting late."

I hesitated. "I'm not sure yet. Give me a little time to get my life in order." My mother gave me a weary look and dropped the subject, but not for long. "Have you applied *any place* for a job?" she asked a few days later. I couldn't blame her since she knew I needed money for my senior year of college. I said nothing and walked away. Each day I waited for the mailman. *Please let me hear something today.*

In the middle of June, my parents' tone changed. We were seated in the living room when they brought up the subject again. This time it was my father who spoke. "Tomorrow you need to begin applying for work. You are letting too much time go by." It was obvious my father wanted action.

I knew it was time for me to tell them about my dilemma. "Actually, I put in an application for a camp job in New York, and I think I'm supposed to work there. That's why I've been hesitating to apply elsewhere. But I haven't heard back. I haven't even received a form rejection letter."

My parents looked surprised. My father glanced at my mother, and then came right to the point. "First thing tomorrow, you give them a call and say you need to know one way or the other. You can't wait any longer." The conversation was over, and I went to bed where I tossed and turned all night long.

The next morning, after a few deep breaths and prayers, I located the number for YDI and called. I was transferred around, but I finally connected with the right person. "Why, Karen, it's so great you called," the woman replied. "I have your application in front of me. We thought we had mailed you a contract to work for us, but we just found the letter buried under a stack of papers. Could you come to New York next week?"

Within a week, I was packed and on a bus to New York. When I finally arrived in the city, I had to pinch myself. The summer flew by, and I was happier than I had ever been. I didn't want it to end. I not only loved being in the city, but I also developed a growing appreciation for upstate New York with its mountains and fast-moving rivers. It was more beautiful than I had imagined.

I cried when I had to leave. Although I returned to Georgetown for my senior year of college and then attended graduate school in Texas, my dream never died. Sometimes God puts a place such as China or India on someone's heart, but for me it was New York, and I kept praying for a chance to return. When a job opened up in the city, I was pinching myself once again. Returning to New York felt so *right*.

I lived and worked in the city for four years until I met and married my husband, John, who wasn't a New York City man, but a New York State man. He was a professor at a college in Oswego, which is a beautiful little town on the banks of Lake Ontario. Winter days could be quite a challenge. Oswego didn't have the hustle and bustle of the city, but it had a peace and quiet I came to love.

We raised our children there and were active in a Bible study group that eventually became a dynamic church. We lived in Oswego for more than thirty years, and I was content. New York had proved to be more than I had ever imagined. I knew I was where I belonged. After all, God had implanted His dream in my heart and then brought it to pass.

—*Karen Reno Knapp*

Riding Through
the Fear

*Jesus said to her, "I am the resurrection and
the life. He who believes in me will live, even
though he dies; and whoever lives and believes
in me will never die. Do you believe this?"*

John 11:25–26

On a seemingly perfect October afternoon in 2006, my husband and I were one of nine couples from Olathe, Kansas, who jumped on motorcycles bound for Branson, Missouri. We had been planning the trip for weeks, looking forward to winding along some of Missouri's spectacular curves and hills, something we don't see a lot of in Kansas. We rode in three separate groups; our group had five bikes, with one couple per bike. The second group, with three couples, left earlier in the day, and the final couple traveled alone.

We had arranged to meet in a hotel in Branson by nightfall. Like most fall days, the air was cool and crisp. We were extremely grateful that the sun was shining that morning, warming us comfortably under our leather gear. After a couple hours on the road, we stopped for fuel and took a much-needed break. Stretching our legs every hundred miles or so was a rejuvenating must, but with dusk approaching, we knew we didn't have time to linger, so we were back on our way in no time.

As we traveled along the two-lane road, we were astonished to see the group with three bikes at an intersection, rounding the corner just ahead of us. Laughing and waving, we called out greetings through CB radios and our group fell in effortlessly behind theirs. The eight bikes graced the road in a precisely staggered formation, an impressive site to the passersby. Unfortunately, we got stuck behind an oversized tractor. Most anyone who travels two-lane country roads has encountered this at one time or another and understands the frustration of going around. Eventually, all the bikes managed to pass and we attempted to regain speed, but something was about to change our lives forever.

A compact car heading toward us in the opposite lane had stopped in order to make a left-hand turn. As the car waited, the driver of a pickup truck evidently did not see it stopped. In a matter of seconds, the truck barreled squarely into the back of the car, slamming it into our line of bikes. Four bikes made it through, but the fifth was struck. The sixth motorcycle went down trying to avoid the debris, another bike was behind it, and we brought up the tail end as bike number eight.

Before I realized what had happened, my husband pulled off the road, shouting into the CB, "Man down—call 911." He jumped off the bike and ran toward the wreckage to assess the scene. He was a trained paramedic and taught to react quickly. I crawled off the bike and stood in a daze, trying to process the whole thing in my head. I did not see the actual hit, only the debris flying afterward, but my husband had seen it all. I was reluctant to approach the site, afraid of what I would find.

God was truly miraculous that day. Not only did we have a paramedic among us, but also another member of our group was a retired highway patrol officer. We believe that their quick reaction and professionalism, along with the efforts of many others, spared the lives of the two motorcycle victims. The drivers of the car and the truck sustained only minor injuries.

Each of us assumed different roles. Some made phone calls to loved ones, some gathered debris that had flown yards from the crash, some helped with traffic control that was building up quickly, and others knelt down and prayed. Darkness was approaching, and the weather was quickly cooling down.

We were only thirty miles from Branson, but the closest trauma center was in Springfield, another seventy miles away. Our friends had to be loaded into ambulances and driven a short distance to the helipad. From there, flight medics transferred them into helicopters and rushed them to Cox South Hospital in Springfield. There we waited, on a road in the middle of nowhere, cold and shaking.

The driver of the bike who went down to avoid debris was taken to a nearby hospital and treated for broken ribs. Most of us stayed at a local hotel until he was released, but one couple rode on to Springfield. They were joined by the final couple from our group, and the four of them went on to the trauma center. There, they provided invaluable support to the victims' family as they trickled in.

Early the next morning, we had one thing on our minds—getting to Springfield, Missouri. The weather had turned bitterly cold. For me, that ride was the most difficult thing I've ever had to do. We were at the emergency room for hours, calling family, comforting one another, praying, and waiting. It was touch and go for quite some time. The female victim was clinically dead on two different occasions, but God obviously wasn't finished with her, because she was revived on both occasions. Although she and her husband have always been incredibly strong individuals, they endured great trials as a result of the accident.

The weather changed upon our return home. My husband and I are fair-weather riders and don't necessarily enjoy riding when frostbite is a potential factor, so I had several months to evaluate my emotions. Our motorcycle club was a tremendous source of support. We met regularly to talk and kept our friends in constant prayer. There were some from the group who said they wouldn't ride again, but I thought I was handling everything okay. I certainly didn't think I would have a problem returning to the bike in the spring, but the first nice day was nothing like I expected.

Excited by the prospect of our first ride, I slipped into my boots, grabbed a light jacket, put on my helmet, and got on the bike. Surprisingly, my heart started racing, and I gripped the handles until my knuckles turned white. I wanted to ride, so what was happening? I couldn't relax, and I flinched at every curve. The hobby I had once enjoyed with my husband was now causing me to suffer a panic attack.

With the advent of warmer weather, I began to walk outside where I brought the problem before

God. I asked Him to help me overcome my fear, although I wasn't absolutely sure what was causing my anxiety. I continued my talks with Him, and then, one day, three little words just popped into my head. I knew it was God. "Listen to me," was all He said.

I felt completely confused. I listened in church, I read my devotions, but I didn't understand. Where was God going with this? The words hung over me for days. Finally, I had an idea. What better way than to load up my iPod and listen as I walked. It seemed simple enough—familiar songs of praise and verses filled with His promises. There was something about the music playing so close to my heart and penetrating my entire body, as I walked alone in those early morning hours. It became a true worship experience for me. I was constantly reminded of God's greatness and of His promises, and I began to look forward to my time alone with Him every morning. Despite these wonderful blessings, I was still overcome with anxiety when I rode the motorcycle. I wanted to ride and I didn't want to be full of fear.

Then a peculiar thing happened. One morning, as I walked, the battery in my iPod went dead. Frustrated, I took off the earphones, and one of the songs immediately came to mind. The words seemed more powerful than ever. "Even though I walk in the shadow of death, I will fear no evil, for my God is with me, whom then shall I fear?" These words were straight from the Psalms. Then, I heard two distinct questions, as if someone walking beside me had spoken aloud. "You know my promises, but do you believe them? Do you believe them for you?"

Suddenly, my mind was bombarded with the lyrics from the songs I had been listening to over and over. God's words raced through my mind. "Do I believe them for me?" I said and stopped for a moment to catch my breath. "Yes. Yes, I do!" I admitted at last. "Whom then shall I fear?" I said with a powerful sense of gratitude and relief.

I can't say that a nervous thought doesn't occur to me from time to time when I get on the motorcycle, but I couldn't continue to live in fear. I knew I had to put my life totally in His hands. When I concentrated on earthly fears, I wasn't putting all my faith in Him. Some day, I will live forever in Heaven with Jesus and my fears will be gone forever, but until then, I'll just keep singing my songs.

—*Jennie Hilligus*

Contributors

Sonja M. Anderson lives in Seattle with her husband and two daughters. She works in the library at her daughter's elementary school.

Sandi L. Banks is Mom/Gramma to nine young ladies. Her stories appear in *A Cup of Comfort® for Mothers* and *A Cup of Comfort® Book of Prayer*. Visit her website at *www.anchorsof hope.com*.

Alma Barkman of Winnipeg, Manitoba, Canada, is a freelance writer and author of seven books. Visit her website at *www.alma barkman.com*.

Evangeline Ruth Beals is a freelance writer. Her two daughters, a dog, and two cats make her home an exciting place to be.

LeAnne Blackmore is a retreat and conference speaker. She and her family live in East Tennessee.

Connie Sturm Cameron has been married to Chuck for thirty years. She is a speaker and the author of *God's Gentle Nudges*. Visit her website at *www.conniecameron.com*.

LeAnn Campbell has published 1,300 articles and coauthored a book of devotionals. She has six children, eleven grandchildren, and two great-grandsons.

Monica Cane is a freelance writer with articles in magazines nationwide. She lives in Northern California with her husband and children.

Kendis Chenoweth is a minister's wife, mother of two, and a passionate communicator of her favorite topic—Jesus Christ.

Holly Packard Cobb is a business consultant, speaker, and writer. She has four children and her husband is pastor of The Church of St. Clement in El Paso, Texas.

Nancy Osterholm Cox is a freelance writer and editor. She is married to her best friend, Scott, and they have three boys.

Katherine J. Crawford and her husband, Gary, live in Omaha, Nebraska. She writes to share God's love with the next generation.

Tracy Crump lives in Mississippi with her husband, Stan. Her work appears in *Focus on the Family, Today's Christian, Pray!,* and others.

Midge DeSart is a wife, mother, and grandmother. She is the author of *Maintaining Balance in a Stress-Filled World.*

Elsi Dodge is a single woman who travels in a thirty-foot RV with her beagle and cat. Visit her website at *www.RVTourist .com.*

Connie Hilton Dunn is a wife, mother, systems specialist, author, and short-term missionary. She and her husband live in Kansas City. Visit her website at *www.shoutlife.com/connie_dunn.*

Liz Hoyt Eberle's work appears in anthologies, including *Life Savors, All Is Calm,* and several *A Cup of Comfort®* projects. Contact her at *eberle2@hotmail.com.*

Kriss Erickson has been a freelance writer since 1981. She devotes herself to energetic healing, having received Reiki Master training in September 2008.

Rita Stella Galieh is a co-speaker for a Christian radio program. Her first book, *Fire in the Rock,* was published in September 2008. Visit her website at *www.ritastellagalieh.com.*

Renee Gray-Wilburn provides writing and editing services from her home in Colorado Springs, Colorado, where she lives with her husband and three children.

Victoria Hart is a native of the Pacific Northwest and lives in Vancouver, Washington. She has three grown children and seven grandchildren.

Stan Higley is a retired engineer in Fairport, New York. He has contributed two stories to the *A Cup of Comfort®* series.

Jennie Hilligus lives in the Kansas City area. Married for twenty-seven years, she has two adult children and a newly acquired son-in-law.

Nanci G. Huyser and her husband live in Kilgore, Texas, where she is working on a bachelor's degree in English.

Imogene Johnson writes children's short stories, personal experience articles, fiction, poetry, and devotionals. She lives in rural Virginia with her husband, O.W.

Charlotte Kardokus is a member of Oregon Christian Writers and American Christian Fiction Writers. She is working on an inspirational historical romance.

Karla Kassebaum is a freelance writer. Her website, *www.karlakasse baum.com*, offers parents a place to rest, relax, and rejuvenate.

Laurie Klein's award-winning works grace numerous publications. She also wrote the classic praise chorus, "I Love You, Lord."

Karen Reno Knapp enjoys spending time with family. Her articles have been published in *Decision, Florida Today*, and numerous other publications.

Mimi Greenwood Knight is a freelance writer who lives in south Louisiana with her husband, four kids, and a menagerie of animals.

Barbara Kugle is an active member of Southwest Christian Writers' Association. She and her husband live in Bayfield, Colorado.

Susan Lawrence is a freelance writer who has had two books published. She lives with her husband, Gary, near Des Moines, Iowa.

Patricia Lee graduated from the University of Oregon and has written freelance articles for various magazines. She lives with her family in Springfield, Oregon.

L. A. Lindburgh and her family reside in Nebraska near the Omaha metro area. She participates in adult Bible studies and teaches young girls.

Lynn Ludwick is working on her first novel, *The Fix-It Sisters*. She recently received a blue ribbon on one of her quilts.

Elaine Young McGuire's book, *My Missionary Journal*, is now available in Christian bookstores nationwide. Elaine lives in Atlanta with her husband, Jim.

Marcia Alice Mitchell has sold more than 350 articles and short stories as well as a devotional book for family caregivers.

Laurie Modrzejewski lives in southern Maryland, where she enjoys writing, reading, and going on long hikes with her family.

Casey Pitts's husband is a military chaplain. She and her family minister to the families of service members.

Melanie Platt lives near Lafayette, Colorado, with her husband and three dogs. She loves writing, dog training, and meeting new friends.

Connie Pombo is an author, speaker, and founder of Women's Mentoring Ministries in Mt. Joy, Pennsylvania. Visit her website at *www.conniepombo.com.*

Linda Blaine Powell has been married for forty-four years and has two married daughters and four grandchildren.

Shirley A. Reynolds is a freelance writer who enjoys four-wheeling, hiking mountain trails, and listening to the forest. Contact her at *heartprints@netzero.com.*

Beverly Rothgery lives in Loveland, Colorado, with her husband, Glen. She has had a few of her devotional writings published.

Darlene Schacht is a mother of four. She is the editor of *Christian Women Online Magazine* and the author of the humorous book, *The Mom Complex.*

Jeanette and Jim Sharp live in The Woodlands, Texas. They attend Crossroads Baptist Church, while Maggie maintains surveillance on those pesky squirrels.

Molly Smith is a Bible study teacher and jail chaplain. She and her husband, Karl, have three adult children.

Gay Sorensen lives in Olympia, Washington, and writes a monthly column for her church newsletter. Her poems and stories have appeared in several publications.

Michele Starkey and her husband, Keith, live in the Hudson Valley of New York where they enjoy life to the fullest.

Reverend Don Sultz has been active in children's ministry for twenty-seven years. He currently lives with his wife of forty-three years.

Donna Sundblad's works include *Pumping Your Muse*, a creative writing book, and two YA fantasy novels: *Windwalker* and *Beyond the Fifth Gate*. Visit her website at *www.theinkslinger.net*.

Marty Trammell, PhD, is the coauthor of *Redeeming Relationships*. He and his wife, Linda, have three inspiring sons.

Christine P. Wang's stories have been published in A *Cup of Comfort*® *for Christians* and A *Cup of Comfort*® *Book of Prayer*. Contact her at *cpw25@cornell.edu*.

Subject Index

Scripture Index